Crochet Stories

LEWIS CARROLL'S

Alice in WONDERLAND

Pat Olski

Photography by
Gloria Cavallaro

Dover Publications, Inc.
Mineola, New York

Bibliographical Note

Crochet Stories: Lewis Carroll's Alice in Wonderland is a new work, first published by Dover Publications, Inc., in 2016. The story text is taken from a standard abridged version of Lewis Carroll's *Alice in Wonderland*.

International Standard Book Number

ISBN-13: 978-0-486-80734-8
ISBN-10: 0-486-80734-7

Manufactured in the United States
80734701   2016
www.doverpublications.com

Contents

Abbreviations

approx approximately

beg begin, beginning

BL work in back loop of stitch

ch chain

cm centimeters

dc double crochet

dec('d) decrease(d)

FL work in front loop of stitch

foll following

hdc half double crochet

hdc2tog half double crochet 2 stitches together

inc increase

m meter(s)

mm millimeter(s)

pm place marker

rem remain(s)(ing)

rep repeat

rnd round

RS right side

sc single crochet

sc2tog single crochet 2 stitches together

sk skip

sl slip

st(s) stitch(es)

tog together

tr treble crochet

WS wrong side

* repeat directions following *

[ ] repeat directions inside brackets

Magic Ring: When pattern indicates to work into a magic ring, do so as follows: make loop around 2 fingers. Work the indicated number of stitches into the loop. Draw up ends of yarn to tighten. Continue as written.

Crochet Stories

LEWIS CARROLL'S

Alice in WONDERLAND

CHAPTER 1

Down the Rabbit-Hole

ALICE WAS BEGINNING TO GET VERY TIRED of sitting by her sister on the bank and of having nothing to do: once or twice she had peeped into the book her sister was reading, but it had no pictures or conversations in it, "and what is the use of a book," thought Alice, "without pictures or conversations?" Suddenly a White Rabbit with pink eyes ran close by her.

There was nothing so *very* remarkable in that; nor did Alice think it so *very* much out of the way to hear the Rabbit say to itself, "Oh dear! Oh dear! I shall be too late!" but when the Rabbit actually *took a watch out of its waistcoat-pocket* and looked at it, and then hurried on, Alice started to her feet, for it flashed across her mind that she had never before seen a rabbit with either a waistcoat, pocket, or a watch to take out of it, and burning with curiosity, she ran across the field after it, and was just in time to see it pop down a large rabbit-hole under the hedge.

In another moment down went Alice after it, never once considering how in the world she was to get out again . . .

Down, down, down. Would the fall never come to an end? "I wonder how many miles I've fallen by this time?" she said aloud. "I wonder if I shall fall right *through* the earth! How funny it'll seem to come out among the people that walk with their heads downwards! Please, Ma'am, is this New Zealand?" She was trying to curtsey as she spoke —fancy *curtseying* as you're falling through the air—when suddenly, thump! thump! down she came upon a heap of sticks and dry leaves, and the fall was over.

Alice was not a bit hurt. Before her was another long passage, and the White Rabbit was hurrying down it, but when she turned the corner, he was no longer to be seen. She found herself in a long, low hall, lit up by a row of lamps.

There were doors all round the hall, but they were all locked. She wondered how she was ever to get out again.

Suddenly she came upon a little three-legged table, all made of solid glass: there was nothing on it but a tiny golden key, and Alice's first idea was that this might belong to one of the doors of the hall; but alas! either the locks were too large, or the key was too small. However, on the second time round, she came upon a low curtain she had not noticed before, and behind it was a little door about fifteen inches high: she tried the little golden key in the lock, and to her great delight it fit!

Alice opened the door and found that it led into a small passage, not much larger than a rathole: she knelt down and looked along the passage into the loveliest garden you ever saw. How she longed to get out of that dark hall, and wander about among those beds of bright flowers and those cool fountains, but she could not even get her head through the doorway; "and even if my head would go through," thought poor Alice, "it would be of very little use without my shoulders."

When she went back to the table, she found a little bottle on it ("which certainly was not here before," said Alice), and tied round the neck of the bottle was a paper label, with the words *Drink Me* beautifully printed on it in large letters.

Since the bottle was not marked "poison," Alice ventured to taste it, and, finding it very nice, she very soon finished it off. . . .

"What a curious feeling!" said Alice. "I must be shutting up like a telescope!"

And so it was indeed; she was now only ten inches high, and her face brightened up at the thought that she was now the right size for going through the little door into that lovely garden. But when she got to the door, she found that she had forgotten the little golden key, and when she went back to the table for it, she found she could not possibly reach it. She tried her best to climb up one of the legs of the table, but it was too slippery; and when she had tired herself out with trying, the poor little thing sat down and cried.

"Come, there's no use in crying like that!" said Alice to herself rather sharply. She generally gave herself very good advice and was fond of pretending to be two people. "But it's no use now," thought poor Alice, "to pretend to be two people! Why, there's hardly enough of me left to make one respectable person!"

Soon her eye fell on a little glass box that was lying under the table: she opened it, and found in it a very small cake, on which the words *"Eat Me"* were beautifully marked in currants. "Well, I'll eat it," said Alice, "and if it makes me grow larger, I can reach the key; and if it makes me grow smaller I can creep under the door. Which way? Which way?" She set to work, and very soon finished off the cake.

Alice

FINISHED MEASUREMENTS

Height = 7½ in / 19cm

MATERIALS

* Lion Brand Vanna's Choice Baby 3.5oz[100g] / 170yds[156m] (100% acrylic) – one skein each: #098 Lamb or #098 Fisherman (MC), #153 Black (A), #157 Duckie (B), #106 Little Boy Blue (C), #100 White (D)

* Small amount of light pink yarn for cheeks

* Small amount of 6-strand pink embroidery floss for mouth

* Size H-8 (5mm) crochet hook OR SIZE TO OBTAIN GAUGE

* Tapestry needle

* Fiberfill stuffing

GAUGE

14 sc and 17 rows = 4in / 10cm. TAKE TIME TO CHECK GAUGE.

Note: Stuff doll as it is worked to make stuffing easier. Do not stuff arms.

ALICE

Feet

Rnd 1: Using A, 8 sc in magic ring, sl st to join, tighten magic ring, turn – 8 sc.

Rnd 2: Ch 1, [sc in next st, 2 hdc in each of next 2 sts, sc in next st] 2 times, sl st to join, turn – 12 sts.

Rnd 3: Ch 1, [sc in next st, hdc in next st, 2 hdc in each of next 2 sts, hdc in next st, sc in next st] 2 times, sl st to join, turn – 16 sts.

Rnd 4: Ch 1, sc in next 3 sts, [sc in next st, 2 hdc in each of next 3 sts, sc in next st] 2 times, sc in next 3 sts, sl st to join, turn – 22 sts.

Rnd 5: Ch 1, BLsc in next 22 sts, sl st to join, turn – 22 sts.

Body

Rnd 6–11: Using MC, ch 1, sc in each st around, sl st to join, do not turn – 22 sts.

Rnd 12: Ch 1, sc in next 5 sts, sc2tog, sc in next 9 sts, sc2tog, sc in next 4 sts, sl st to join – 20 sc.

Rnd 13: Ch 1, sc in each st around, sl st to join – 20 sc.

Rnd 14: Ch 1, sc in next 4 sts, sc2tog, sc in next 8 sts, sc2tog, sc in next 4 sts, sl st to join – 18 sc.

Rnd 15: Ch 1, sc in each st around, sl st to join – 18 sc.

Rnd 16: Ch 1, sc in next 4 sts, sc2tog, sc in next 7 sts, sc2tog, sc in next 3 sts, sl st to join – 16 sc.

Rnd 17: Ch 1, [sc in next 3 sts, ch 2, sk 2 for armhole, sc in next 3 sts] 2 times, sl st to join.

Rnd 18: Ch 1, [sc in next 3 sts, sc in ch-sp, sc in next 3 sts] 2 times, sl st to join – 14 sc.

Head

Rnd 19: Ch 1, sc in next 2 sts, 2 sc in next st, [sc in next 2 sts, 2 sc in next st] 3 times, sc in next 2 sts, sl st to join – 18 sts.

Rnd 20: Ch 1, sc in next 2 sts, 2 sc in next st, [sc in next 3 sts, 2 sc in next st] 3 times, sc in next 3 sts, sl st to join – 22 sts.

Rnd 21: Ch 1, sc in next 4 sts, 2 sc in next st, [sc in next 4 sts, 2 sc in next st] 3 times, sc in next 2 sts, sl st to join – 26 sts.

Rnd 22: Ch 1, sc in next 2 sts, 2 sc in next st, [sc in next 5 sts, 2 sc in next st] 3 times, sc in next 2 sts, sl st to join – 30 sts.

Rnds 23–25: Ch 1, sc in each st around, sl st to join – 30 sts.

Rnd 26: Ch 1, sc in next 2 sts, sc2tog, [sc in next 6 sts, sc2tog] 3 times, sc in next 2 sts, sl st to join – 26 sts.

Rnd 27: Using B, ch 1, sc in next 4 sts, sc2tog, [sc in next 4 sts, sc2tog] 3 times, sc in next 2 sts, sl st to join – 22 sts.

Rnd 28: Ch 1, sc in next 2 sts, sc2tog, [sc in next 3 sts, sc2tog] 3 times, sc in next 3 sts, sl st to join – 18 sts.

Rnd 29: Ch 1, sc in next 2 sts, sc2tog, [sc in next 2 sts, sc2tog] 3 times, sc in next 2 sts, sl st to join – 14 sts.

Rnd 30: Ch 1, sc in next sc, sc2tog, [sc in next st, sc2tog] 3 times, sc in next 2 sts, sl st to join – 10 sts.

Rnd 31: Ch 1, sc in next sc, sc2tog 4 times, sc in next st, sl st to join – 6 sts. Fasten off, leaving tail. Stuff and sew opening closed.

Arms (make 1)

Rnd 1: Using MC, 4 sc in magic ring, sl st to join, tighten magic ring – 4 sc.

Rnd 2: Ch 1, sc in each st around, sl st to join – 4 sc.

Rnd 3: Using C, ch 1, sc in each st around, sl st to join.

Rnd 4: Ch 1, [sc in next st, 2 sc in next st] 2 times, sl st to join – 6 sc.

Rnd 5, 13: Ch 1, [sc in next st, 2 sc in next st] 3 times, sl st to join – 9 sc.

Rnds 6–8, 10–12, 14–16: Ch 1, sc in each st around, sl st to join.

Rnds 9, 17: Ch 1, [sc in next st, sc2tog] 3 times, sl st to join – 6 sc.

Rnd 18: Ch 1, [sc in next st, sc2tog] 2 times, sl st to join – 4 sc.

Rnds 19–20: Using MC, ch 1, sc in each st around, sl st to join. Fasten off, leaving a long tail.

Dress Bodice (worked flat)

Row 1 (RS) : Using D, ch 23, sc in 2nd ch from hook and each st across, turn – 22 sc.

Row 2 (WS) : Ch 1, FLsc in next 4 sts, ch 3, sk 3 sts for armhole, FLsc in next 8 sts, ch 3, sk 3 sts for armhole, FLsc in next 4 sts, turn – 22 sc.

Row 3: Ch 1, BLsc in next 4 sts, sc in each of next 3 ch, BLsc in next 8 sts, sc in each of next 3 ch, BLsc in next 4 sts, turn – 22 sc.

Row 4: Ch 1, sc in each st across, turn – 22 sc.

Row 5: Ch1, BLsc in next 3 sts [2 BLsc in next st, BLsc in next 4 sts] 3 times, 2 BLsc in next st, BLsc in next 3 sts, turn – 26 sts.

Row 6: Ch 1, sc in each st across, do not turn.

Skirt

Rnd 7: Sl st in first st to join to work in rnds, ch 1, turn work so that the right side is facing, BLsc in next 3 sts, [2 BLsc in next st, BLsc in next 4 sts] 4 times, 2 BLsc in next st, BLsc in next 2 sts, sl st to join – 31 sts.

Rnd 8: Ch 1, BLsc in each st around, sl st to join.

Rnd 9: Ch 1, BLsc in next 3 sts, [2 BLsc in next st, BLsc in next 4 sts] 5 times, 2 Blsc in next st, BLsc in next 2 sts, sl st to join – 37 sts.

Rnd 10: Ch 1, BLsc in each st around, sl st to join.

Rnd 11: Ch 1, BLsc in next 36 sts, 2 BLsc in next st, sl st to join – 38 sts.

Rnd 12: (Work all sts in FL) [(sl st, ch 2, sl st) in next sc, sl st in next sc] around, sl st to join, fasten off – 19 picots.

Rnd 13: Using C, working behind Rnd 12, BLsc in each st of Rnd 11, sl st to join – 37 sc.

Rnd 14: ch1, sc in each st around, sl st to join, fasten off.

FINISHING

Arms

Thread tapestry needle with yarn tail and close up ring at bottom of arm. Pull arm piece through armholes, centering it so arms are of equal length. Weave in all ends.

Dress

Weave in ends. Place dress on doll and sew back opening closed.

Bow

Using A, ch 24, sc in 2nd ch from hook and each ch across, fasten off – 23 sc.

Tie bow and sew to front of dress.

Hair

Wrap B around a 9in/23cm piece of cardboard 70 times. Using a separate strand of B, work 8 sc through the wrapped yarn to secure the fringe; fasten off. Cut the fringe, being careful to keep the 2 sides separate. Remove the cardboard. Sew hair to doll's head through the row of sc. Trim hair.

Headband

Using D, ch 30, sc in 2nd ch from hook and each ch across, fasten off – 29 sc.

Wrap headband around head and secure underneath.

Face

Using tapestry needle and A, embroider eyes by working 2 lazy daisy sts, one inside the other. Cheeks are made the same way with lt pink yarn. Then, sew a small white stitch in the top of each eye. The mouth is embroidered with pink floss, with a straight stitch secured in the middle using another straight stitch as illustrated.

SKILL LEVEL
Easy

FINISHED MEASUREMENTS

Height = 5in/13cm

MATERIALS

* Lion Brand Vanna's Choice 3.5oz[100g]/170yds[156m] (100% acrylic) – one skein each: #098 Lamb (MC), #153 Black (A), #157 Duckie (B), #106 Little Boy Blue (C), #100 White (D)

* Small amounts of 6-strand embroidery floss in pink for mouth and cheeks and black for eyes

* Size H-8 (5mm) crochet hook OR SIZE TO OBTAIN GAUGE

* Tapestry needle

* Fiberfill stuffing

GAUGE

14 sc and 17 rows = 4in/10cm. TAKE TIME TO CHECK GAUGE.

Note: Stuff doll as it is worked to make stuffing easier. Do not stuff arms.

SMALL ALICE

Feet

Rnd 1: Using A, 8 sc in magic ring, sl st to join, tighten magic ring, turn – 8 sc.

Rnd 2: Ch 1, [sc in next 3 sts, 2 sc in next st] 2 times, sl st to join, turn – 10 sts.

Rnd 3: Ch 1, [sc in next 3 sts, 2 sc in each of next 2 sts] 2 times, sl st to join, turn – 14 sts.

Rnd 4: Ch 1, BLsc in each st around, sl st to join, turn.

Dress Hem

Rnds 5–6: Using C, ch 1, sc in each st around, sl st to join, turn – 14 sts.

Apron

Rnds 7–9: Using D, ch 1, BLsc in each st around, sl st to join, do not turn.

Rnd 10: Ch 1, [BLsc in next 5 sts, BLsc2tog] 2 times, sl st to join – 12 sts.

Rnd 11: Ch 1, BLsc in next st, ch 2, sk 1 for armhole, BLsc in next 5 sts, ch 2, sk 1 for armhole, Blsc in next 4 sts, sl st to join.

Head

Rnd 12: Using MC, ch 1, Blsc in next st, sc in ch-sp, BLsc in next 5 sts, sc in ch-sp, BLsc in next 4 sts, sl st to join – 12 sts.

Rnd 13: Ch 1, [sc in next 2 sts, 2 sc in next st] 4 times, sl st to join – 16 sts.

Rnd 14: Ch 1, [sc in next 3 sts, 2 sc in next st] 4 times, sl st to join – 20 sts.

Rnd 15: Ch 1, sc in each st around, sl st to join – 20 sts.

Rnd 16: Ch 1, [sc in next 3 sts, sc2tog] 4 times, sl st to join – 16 sts.

Rnd 17: Ch 1, [sc in next 2 sts, sc2tog] 4 times, sl st to join – 12 sts.

Rnd 18: Using B, ch1, [sc in next st, sc2tog] 4 times, sl st to join – 8 sts.

Rnd 19: Ch 1, sc2tog 4 times, sl st to join – 4sts. Fasten off, leaving tail. Stuff and sew opening closed.

Arms (make 1)

Rnd 1: Using MC, 4 sc in magic ring, sl st to join, tighten magic ring, – 4 sc.

Rnds 2, 4–13: Using C, ch 1, sc in each st around, sl st to join.

Rnd 3: Ch 1, [2 sc in next sc, sc in next st] 2 times, sl st to join – 6 sc.

Rnd 14: Ch 1, [sc in next st, sc2tog] 2 times, sl st to join – 4 sc.

Rnd 15: Using MC, ch 1, sc in each st around, sl st to join – 4 sc. Fasten off, leaving tail; sew opening closed.

Bow

Using A, ch 20, fasten off. Weave in ends. Fold into a bow shape and sew to front of dress.

FINISHING

Arms

Pull arm piece through armholes, centering it so arms are of equal length. Weave in all ends.

Hair

Wrap B around a 6in / 15cm piece of cardboard 50 times. Using a separate strand of B, sc 5 sts through wrapped yarn to secure. Fasten off. Cut loops, being careful to keep the sides separated. Remove from cardboard. Place hair on head with sc side facing down and sew to head. Trim hair.

Headband

Using D, ch 20, fasten off. Wrap headband around head and secure underneath.

Face

Use black floss to embroider eyes by working 2 lazy daisy sts, and a French knot, one inside the other. Cheeks are made the same way with light pink floss. Embroider mouth with darker pink floss, with a straight stitch secured in the middle using another straight stitch.

White Rabbit

FINISHED MEASUREMENTS

Height (to top of ears) = 9in/23cm

MATERIALS

* Lion Brand Vanna's Choice 3.5oz[100g]/170yds[156m](100% acrylic) – one skein each: #100 White (MC), #102 Aqua (A), #132 Radiant Orange (B), small amounts of #101 Pink (C)

* Black 6-strand embroidery floss for teeth

* Size H-8 (5mm) crochet hook OR SIZE TO OBTAIN GAUGE

* Tapestry needle

* Fiberfill stuffing

* Watch charm

GAUGE

14 sc and 17 rows = 4in/10cm. TAKE TIME TO CHECK GAUGE.

Note: Stuff doll as it is worked to make stuffing easier. Do not stuff arms.

WHITE RABBIT

Feet

Rnd 1: Using MC, 8 sc in magic ring, sl st to join, tighten magic ring, turn – 8 sc.

Rnd 2: Ch 1, [sc in next st, 2 hdc in each of next 2 sts, sc in next st] 2 times, sl st to join, turn – 12 sts.

Rnd 3: Ch 1, [sc in next st, hdc in next st, 2 hdc in each of next 2 sts, hdc in next st, sc in next st] 2 times, sl st to join, turn – 16 sts.

Rnd 4: Ch 1, sc in next 3 sts, [sc in next st, 2 hdc in each of next 3 sts, sc in next st] 2 times, sc in next 3 sts, sl st to join, turn – 22 sts.

Rnd 5: Ch 1, BLsc in each st around, sl st to join, do not turn.

Rnds 6–7: Ch 1, sc in each st around, sl st to join.

Body

Rnd 8: Using A, ch 1, sc in each st around, sl st to join.

Rnd 9: Ch 1, sc in next 2 sts, *sc in next st, [2 sc in next st, sc in next 2 sts] 3 times, rep from *, sl st to join – 28 sts.

Rnds 10–12: Ch 1, sc in each st around, sl st to join.

Rnd 13: Ch 1, sc in next 2 sts, *sc in next st, [sc-2tog, sc in next 2 sts] 3 times, rep from *, sl st to join – 22 sts.

Rnd 14: Ch 1, sc in each st around, sl st to join.

Rnd 15: Ch 1, sc in next 5 sts, sc2tog, sc in next 9 sts, sc2tog, sc in next 4 st, sl st to join – 20 sts.

Rnd 16: Using MC, ch 1, [sc in next 4 sts, sc2tog, sc in next 4 sts] 2 times, sl st to join – 18 sc.

Rnd 17: Ch 1, sc in next 4 sts, sc2tog, sc in next 7 sts, sc2tog, sc in next 3 sts, sl st to join – 16 sc.

Rnd 18: Ch 1, [sc in next 3 sts, ch 2, sk 2 for arm-hole, sc in next 3 sts] 2 times, sl st to join.

Rnd 19: Ch 1, [sc in next 3 sts, sc in ch-sp, sc in next 3 sts] 2 times, sl st to join – 14 sc.

Head

Rnd 20: Ch 1, [sc in next 2 sts, 2 sc in next st] 4 times, sc in next 2 sts, sl st to join – 18 sts.

Rnd 21: Ch 1, [sc in next 3 sts, 2 sc in next st] 4 times, sc in next 2 sts, sl st to join – 22 sts.

Rnd 22: Ch 1, [sc in next 4 sts, 2 sc in next st] 4 times, sc in next 2 sts, sl st to join – 26 sts.

Rnd 23: Ch 1, sc in next 2 sts, 2 sc in next st, [sc in next 6 sts, 2 sc in next st] 3 times, sc in next 2 sts, sl st to join – 30 sts.

Rnds 24–26: Ch 1, sc in each st around, sl st to join – 30 sts.

Rnd 27: Ch 1, sc in next 2 sts, sc2tog, [sc in next 6 sts, sc2tog] 3 times, sc in next 2 sts, sl st to join –26 sts.

Rnd 28: Ch 1, [sc in next 4 sts, sc2tog] 4 times, sc in next 2 sts, sl st to join – 22 sts.

Rnd 29: Ch 1, sc in next 2 sts, sc2tog, [sc in next 3 sts, sc2tog] 3 times, sc in next 3 sts, sl st to join – 18 sts.

Rnd 30: Ch 1, [sc in next 2 sts, sc2tog] 4 times, sc in next 2 sts, sl st to join – 14 sts.

Rnd 31: Ch 1, sc in each st around, sl st to join – 14 sts.

Rnd 32: Ch 1, [sc in next st, sc2tog] 4 times, sc in next 2 sts, sl st to join – 10 sts.

Rnd 33: Ch 1, sc in each st around, sl st to join – 10 sts.

Rnd 34: Ch 1, sc in next st, sc2tog 4 times, sc in next st, sl st to join – 6 sts. Fasten off, leaving tail. Stuff and sew opening closed.

Arms (make 1)

Rnd 1: Using MC, 4 sc in magic ring, sl st to join, tighten magic ring, turn – 4 sc.

Rnds 2–3: Ch 1, sc in each st around, sl st to join.

Rnd 4: Ch 1, [sc in next st, 2 sc in next st] 2 times, sl st to join – 6 sc.

Rnds 5, 13: Ch 1, [sc in next st, 2 sc in next st] 3 times, sl st to join – 9 sc.

Rnds 6-8, 10-12, 14-16: Ch 1, sc in each st around, sl st to join.

Rnds 9, 17: Ch 1, [sc in next st, sc2tog] 3 times, sl st to join – 6 sc.

Rnd 18: Ch 1, [sc in next st, sc2tog] 2 times, sl st to join – 4 sc.

Rnds 19–20: Ch 1, sc in each st around, sl st to join. Fasten off, leaving a long tail.

Vest (work from top down)

Row 1 (RS) : Using B, ch 23, sc in 2nd ch from hook and each st across, turn – 22 sc.

Row 2: Ch 1, sc in next 4 sts, ch 3, sk 3 for arm-hole, sc in next 8 sts, ch 3, sk 3 for armhole, sc in next 4 sts, sl st to join, turn.

Row 3: Ch 1, sc in next 4 sts, sc in next 3 chs, sc in next 8 sts , sc in next 3 chs, sc in next 4 sts , sl st to join, turn.

Row 4: Ch 1, sc in each st across, turn.

Row 5: Ch 1, sc in next 3 sts, [2 sc in next st, sc in next 4 sts] 3 times, 2 sc in next st, sc in next 3 sts, turn – 26 sts.

Row 6: Ch 1, sc in each st across, turn.

Row 7: Ch 1, sc in next 8 sts, hdc in next st, dc in next st, hdc in next st, sc in next st, sl st in next 2 sts, sc in next st, hdc in next st, dc in next st, hdc in next st, sc in next 8 sts, fasten off.

Bowtie

Row 1: Using A, ch 5, sc in 2nd ch from hook and each st across, turn – 4 sc.

Row 2: Ch 1, sc in each st across. Fasten off, leaving long tail to sew to doll. Weave one thread in and wrap around the center of the crocheted piece to make a bow shape.

Ears (make 2)

Inner Ear

Using C, ch 9, sc in 2nd ch from hook and each st across. Fasten off, leaving long tail for sewing.

Outer Ear

Rnd 1: Using MC, ch 17, sc in 2nd ch from hook and each st across, ch 1. Working in base of ch, sc in next 16 sts – 33 sts.

Rnd 2: Ch 1, sc in next 16 sts. Fasten off, leaving long tail for sewing.

FINISHING

Arms

Use tapestry needle to close up ring at bottom of arm. Pull arm piece through armholes, centering it so arms are of equal length, and sew in place. Weave in all ends.

Head

Use tapestry needle and embroidery floss to embroider the eyes and mouth. Sew pink inner ear pieces to outer parts of ear. Sew ears to the back of the head as illustrated. They are long so that they can be anchored to the back and not "wilt."

Knot five strands of white yarn to the top of the head. Trim the hair and fluff with a needle to make the center tuft.

Legs

Using MC, shape bottom of legs with a few straight stitches.

Vest

Using a 6-strand length of black embroidery floss, embroider French knot buttons and sew watch onto vest. Place vest on doll and close back seam. Tie bowtie around neck.

Tail

Make pompom—wrap MC around 3 fingers fifteen times. Tie in center with a separate piece of yarn. Cut loops, trim to desired size, and fluff fiber with tapestry needle. Sew to back of rabbit.

Face

Use 2 strands of embroidery floss to embroider teeth. Work 2 large straight stitches using pink yarn for the mouth. Embroider eyes using black yarn, by making 2 lazy daisy sts, one inside the other. Embroider cheeks the same way, using lt pink yarn. Embroider the mouth with one straight st over the teeth.

Bottle

FINISHED MEASUREMENTS

Height = $5^1/_2$ in / 14cm

MATERIALS

* Lion Brand Vanna's Choice 3.5oz[100g] / 170yds[156m] (100% acrylic) – one skein each: #172 Kelly Green (MC), #123 Beige (A)

* Size H-8 (5mm) crochet hook OR SIZE TO OBTAIN GAUGE

* Tapestry needle

* Fiberfill stuffing

GAUGE

14 sc and 17 rows = 4in / 10cm. TAKE TIME TO CHECK GAUGE.

Note: Stuff piece as it is worked to make stuffing easier.

BOTTLE

Rnd 1: Using MC, 4 sc in magic ring, sl st to join, tighten magic ring – 4 sc.

Rnds 2–3: Ch 1, 2 sc in each st around, sl st to join – 16 sc.

Rnd 4: Ch 1, BLsc in each st around, sl st to join.

Rnds 5–15: Ch 1, sc in each st around, sl st to join.

Rnd 16: Ch 1 [BLsc in next 2 sts, BLsc2tog] around 4 times, sl st to join – 12 sc.

Rnd 17: Ch 1, [sc in next st, sc2tog] around 4 times, sl st to join – 8 sc.

Rnds 18–19: Ch 1, sc in each st around, sl st to join.

Rnd 20: Using A, ch 1, BLsc in each st around, sl st to join.

Rnd 21: Ch 1, sc in each st around, sl st to join.

Rnd 22: Ch 1, BLsc2tog 4 times, sl st to join – 4 sc. Fasten off, leaving tail. Stuff and sew opening closed. Weave in ends.

Tip: Use materials of your choice to create a label if desired.

Cake

FINISHED MEASUREMENTS

Height = 2in/5cm

Circumference = 11 ¼ in/29cm

MATERIALS

* Lion Brand Vanna's Choice 3.5oz[100g]/170yds[156m] (100% acrylic) – one skein each: #124 Toffee (MC), #100 White (A), small amounts of #101 Pink (B), #141 Wild Berry (C) and #172 Kelly Green (D)

* Size H-8 (5mm) crochet hook OR SIZES TO OBTAIN GAUGE

* Stitch marker

* Tapestry needle

* Fiberfill stuffing

GAUGE

14 sc and 17 rows = 4in/10cm. TAKE TIME TO CHECK GAUGE.

STITCH GLOSSARY

MB (Make Bobble): Insert hook in st, pull up lp, yarn over, insert hook in same st, pull up another loop, yarn over and draw through all 4 lps on hook.

Note: Stuff piece as it is worked to make stuffing easier.

CAKE

Rnd 1: Using MC, 4 sc in magic ring, sl st to join, tighten magic ring – 4 sc.

Rnds 2–3: Ch 1, 2 sc in each st around, sl st to join – 16 sc.

Rnds 4–5: Ch 1, [sc in next st, 2 sc in next st] around, sl st to join – 36 sc.

Rnd 6: Ch 1, sc in each st around, sl st to join.

Rnds 7–12: Ch 1, BLsc in each st around, sl st to join.

Place marker (pm) at Rnd 7 to mark bottom rnd.

Tip: Use materials of your choice to create a label if desired.

Rnd 13: Using A, ch 1, BLsc in each st around, sl st to join.

Rnds 14–15: Ch 1, [sc in next st, sc2tog] around, sl st to join – 16 sc.

Rnds 16–17: Ch 1, sc2tog around, sl st to join – 4 sc. Fasten off, leaving tail. Stuff and sew opening closed.

White Icing Trim at Bottom of Cake

Join A to Rnd 7. Work in FL, ch 1, [sl st in next st, MB in next st] around, sl st to join. Fasten off.

Rose

Using B, ch 8, (sl st, ch 1, 2 sc, sl st) in 2nd ch from hook and each ch across. Fasten off, leaving tail. Coil into a flower shape and secure with a couple of sts.

Leaves

Using D, ch 13, sc in 2nd ch from hook, 2 hdc in next st, sc in next st, sl st in next 6 sts, sc in next st, 2 hdc in next st, sc in next st. Fasten off, leaving tail.

FINISHING

Weave in ends. Using C, embroider a French knot in every other sc at top edge of cake. Sew leaves and rose to top of cake as illustrated.

CHAPTER 2
The Pool of Tears

"Curiouser and curiouser!" cried Alice. "Now I'm opening out like the largest telescope that ever was! Good-bye, feet!" (for when she looked down at her feet they seemed to be almost out of sight, they were getting so far off). "Oh, my poor little feet, I wonder who will put on your shoes and stockings for you now, dears?"

Just at this moment her head struck against the roof of the hall: in fact she was now rather more than nine feet high, and she at once took up the little golden key and hurried off to the garden door.

Poor Alice! It was as much as she could do, lying down on one side, to look through into the garden with one eye; but to get through was more hopeless than ever: she sat down and began to cry again.

"You ought to be ashamed of yourself," said Alice, "a great girl like you," (she might well say this), "to go on crying in this way! Stop this moment, I tell you!" But she went on all the same, shedding gallons of tears, until there was a large pool all around her, about four inches deep and reaching halfway down the hall.

After a time she heard a little pattering of feet in the distance, and hastily dried her eyes. It was the White Rabbit returning, with a pair of white kid-gloves in one hand and a large fan in the other. "Oh! The Duchess! the Duchess! Oh! *Won't* she be savage if I've kept her waiting!"

"If you please, Sir—" said Alice. The Rabbit started violently, dropped the white kid-gloves and the fan, and scurried away into the darkness as hard as he could go.

Alice took up the fan and gloves, and as the hall was very hot, she began fanning herself. She was surprised to see that she had put on one of the Rabbit's little white kid-gloves. "How can I have done that?" she thought. "I must be getting small again." She got up and went to the table to measure herself by it; she was now about two feet high, and was shrinking rapidly. She soon found out that the cause of this was the fan she was holding, and she dropped it hastily, just in time to save herself from shrinking away altogether.

"That was a narrow escape!" said Alice. "And now for the garden!" But alas! the little door was shut again, and the little golden key was lying on the glass table as before, "and things are worse than ever," thought the poor child, "for I never was so small as this before, never!"

As she said these words her foot slipped, and in another moment, splash! she was up to her chin in saltwater. Her first idea was that she had fallen into the sea; however, she soon made out that she was in the pool of tears she had wept when she was nine feet high.

"I wish I hadn't cried so much!" said Alice, as she swam about, trying to find her way out. "I shall be punished for it now, I suppose, by being drowned in my own tears!"

Just then she heard something splashing about in the pool a little way off, and she soon made out that it was a mouse, that had slipped in like herself.

"Would it be of any use now," thought Alice, "to speak to this mouse?" She began: "O Mouse, do you know the way out of this pool?" (Alice thought this must be the right way of speaking to a mouse: she remembered having seen, in her brother's Latin Grammar, "A Mouse—of a mouse—to a mouse—O mouse!")

"Perhaps it doesn't understand English," thought Alice. "I daresay it's a French mouse, come over with William the Conqueror." So she began again: "Où est ma chatte?" which was the first sentence in her French lesson-book. The Mouse gave a sudden leap out of the water at this mention of cats, and when Alice spoke about dogs, the Mouse began swimming away from her as hard as it could go.

By now the pool was getting quite crowded with the birds and animals that had fallen into it: a Dodo and an Eaglet, and several other curious creatures. Alice led the way, and the whole party swam to the shore.

Dodo Bird

SKILL LEVEL
Intermediate

FINISHED MEASUREMENTS

Height = 8¹/₂ in / 21cm

MATERIALS

* Universal Yarns Deluxe Worsted 3.5oz[100g]/220yds[200m] (100% wool) – one skein each: #12192 Nitrox Blue (MC), #12270 Natural (A), #12297 Sherbet (B), #12280 Blue Chic (C), small amounts #14013 Shamrock (D) and black yarn

* Size G-6 (4mm) crochet hook OR SIZE TO OBTAIN GAUGE

* Tapestry needle

* Fiberfill stuffing

* Stitch markers

GAUGE

20 sc and 20 rows = 4in/10cm. TAKE TIME TO CHECK GAUGE.

Note: Stuff piece as it is worked to make stuffing easier.

DODO BIRD

Head

Using A, ch 13, sl st to form ring.

Rnd 1: Ch 1, 12 sc in ring, sl st to join – 12 sc.

Rnd 2: Ch 1, [sc in next 2 sts, 2 sc in next st] 4 times, sl st to join – 16 sc.

Rnds 3–6, 13–15, 19: Ch 1, sc in each st around, sl st to join.

Rnd 7: Ch 1, [sc in next st, 2 sc in next st], sc in next 12 sts, [2 sc in next st, sc in next st], sl st to join – 18 sc.

Rnd 8: Ch 1, [2 sc in next st, sc in next 3 sts, 2 sc in next st, sc in next 4 sts] 2 times, sl st to join – 22 sc.

Rnd 9: Using C, ch 1, sc 22, sl st into first sc to close rnd – 22 sc.

Rnd 10: Ch 1, sc in next 2 sts, [2 sc in next st, sc in next 3 sts] 5 times, sl st to join – 27 sc.

Rnd 11: Ch 1, 2 sc in next st, [2 sc in next st, sc in next 4 sts] 5 times, 2 sc in next st, sl st to join – 34 sc.

Rnd 12: Ch 1, [2 sc in next st, sc in next 5 sts] 5 times, 2 sc in next st, sc in next 3 sts, sl st to join – 40 sc.

Rnd 16: Ch 1, [sc2tog, sc in next 6 sts] 5 times, sl st to join – 35 sc.

Rnd 17: Ch 1, sc in next 3 sts [sc2tog, sc in next 4 sts] 5 times, sc2tog, sl st to join – 29 sc.

Rnd 18: Ch 1, sc in next st, [sc2tog, sc in next 2 sts] 7 times, sl st to join – 22 sc.

Rnd 20: Ch 1, [sc in next 2 sts, sc2tog] 5 times, sc in next 2 sts, sl st to join – 17 sc.

Rnd 21: Ch 1, [sc in next 2 sts, sc2tog] 4 times, sc in next st, sl st to join – 13 sc.

Rnd 22: Ch 1, [sc in next st, sc2tog] 4 times, sc in next st, sl st to join – 9 sc.

Rnd 23: Ch 1, sc2tog 4 times, sc in next st, sl st to join – 5 sc. Fasten off, leaving tail. Stuff and sew opening closed.

Body

Using MC, ch 24, sl st to form ring.

Rnd 1: Ch 1, 23 sc in ring, sl st to join – 23 sc.

Rnd 2: Ch 1, sc in next 10 sts, 2 sc in each of next 3 sts, sc in next 10 sts, sl st to join – 26 sc.

Rnds 3, 6, 8–10, 12–14: Ch 1, sc in each st around, sl st to join.

Rnd 4: Ch 1, [sc in next 2 sts, 2 sc in next st] 3 times, sc in next 7 sts, [2 sc in next st, sc in next 2 sts] 3 times, sk next st, sl st to join – 31 sc.

Rnd 5: Ch 1, [sc in next 2 sts, 2 sc in next st] 4 times, sc in next 7 sts, [2 sc in next st, sc in next 2 sts] 4 times, sl st to join – 39 sc.

Rnd 7: Ch 1, [sc in next 2 sts, 2 sc in next st] 4 times, sc in next 15 sts, [2 sc in next st, sc in next 2 sts] 4 times, sl st to join – 47 sc.

Rnd 11: Ch 1, [sc in next 2 sts, 2 sc in next st] 4 times, sc in next 23 sts, [2 sc in next st, sc in next 2 sts] 4 times, sl st to join – 55 sc.

Rnd 15: Ch 1, BLsc in each st around, sl st to join.

Rnd 16: Ch 1, [sc in next 2 sts, sc2tog] 3 times, [sc in next 3 sts, sc2tog] 6 times, [sc in next 2 sts, sc2tog] 3 times, sc in next st, sl st to join – 43 sc.

Rnd 17: Ch 1, sc in next 11 sts, [sc2tog, sc in next 2 sts] 2 times, sc2tog, sc in next st, [sc2tog, sc in next 2 sts] 3 times, sc in next 9 sts, sl st to join – 37 sc.

Rnd 18: Ch 1, sc in next 9 sts, [sc2tog, sc in next st] 2 times, sc2tog, sc in next 3 sts, [sc2tog, sc in next st] 2 times, sc2tog, sc in next 9 sts, sl st to join – 31 sc.

Begin short row shaping.

Row 19: Sc2tog 2 times, sc in next 5 sts, turn, ch 1, sc in next 12 sts, sc2tog, turn, ch 1, sc in next 7 sts, ending at center back do not turn – 27 sts.

Row 20: Sc in next 7 sts, sc2tog, sc in next st, sc2tog, sc in next 3 sts, sc2tog , sc in next st, sc2tog, sc in next 7 sts – 23 sts.

Row 21: Sc2tog, sc in next 5 sts, sc2tog, sc in next st, sc3tog, sc in next st, sc2tog, sc in next 5 sts, sc2tog – 17 sts.

Row 22: Sc2tog 2 times, sc in next 2 sts, sc2tog, sc in next st, sc2tog, sc in next 2 sts, sc2tog 2 times – 11sts.

Row 23: Sc2tog 2 times, sc3tog, sc2tog 2 times –5 sts. Fasten off, leaving tail. Stuff and sew opening closed.

Beak

Rnd 1: Using B, 4 sc in magic ring, sl st to join, tighten magic ring – 4 sc.

Rnd 2: Ch 1, [sc in next st, 2 sc in next st] 2 times, sl st to join – 6 sc.

Rnd 3: Ch 1, [sc in next 2 sts, 2 sc in next st] 2 times, sl st to join – 8 sc.

Row 4: Ch 1, sc in next 2 sts, 2 sc in next st, sc in next 2 sts, 2 sc in next st, sc in next 2 sts, do not join, turn – 10 sc.

Rows 5–6: Ch 1, sc in each st across, turn.

Row 7: Ch 1, [sc in next st, sc2tog] 3 times, sc in next st, turn – 7 sc.

Row 8: Ch 1, [sc in next st, sc2tog] 2 times, sc in next st, – 5 sc. Fasten off, leaving tail; sew to head.

Feet (make 2)

Rnd 1: Using B, 5 sc in magic ring, sl st to join, tighten magic ring – 5 sc.

Rnd 2: Ch 1, [ch 4, turn, sc in 2nd chain from hook and in next 2 chs, sc in next st] 2 times, ch 4, turn, sc in 2nd ch and in next 2 chs, 2 sc in next st, sl st to join, fasten off.

Legs (make 1)

Row 1: Using B, ch 31, sc in 2nd ch from hook and each st across, turn – 30 sc.

Row 2: Ch 1, sc in each st across. Fold piece in half lengthwise, sl st long edges tog, fasten off, leaving tail; sew a foot to each end.

Wings (make 2)

Rnd 1: Using C, 3 sc in magic ring, sl st to join, tighten magic ring – 3 sc.

Row 2: Ch 1, sc in next st, 2 sc in next st, sc in next st, turn, do not join – 4 sc.

Row 3: Ch 1, sc in next st, 2 sc in each of next 2 sc, sc in next st, turn – 6 sc.

Row 4: Ch 1, sc in next 2 sts, 2 sc in each of next 2 sc, sc in next 2 sts, turn – 8 sc.

Row 5: Using D, ch 1, sc in each st across, turn.

Row 6: Ch 1, sc in next st, 2 sc in next st, sc in next 4 sts, 2 sc in next st, sc in next st, turn – 10 sc.

Rows 7–8: Ch 1, sc in each st across, turn. Fasten off.

FINISHING

Sew beak to head. Sew head to body. Fold leg piece in half and center under body, stitch in place.

Sew wings to side of body. Weave in ends. Use black yarn to make 2 French knot eyes.

Head tufts (make 2)

Cut 6in/15cm pieces of B, C, and D. Fold in half and knot through top of head. Rep for 2nd tuft. Use blunt tip of tapestry needle to tease yarn gently and separate the plies.

CHAPTER 3

A Caucus-Race and a Long Tale

The first question was how they were all to get dry again: the birds and animals had a consultation about this, and after a few minutes it seemed quite natural to Alice to find herself talking familiarly with them.

At last the Mouse, who seemed to be a person of some authority among them, called out, "Sit down, all of you, and listen to me! I'll soon make you dry enough!" They all sat down in a large ring, with the Mouse in the middle.

"Are you all ready?" the Mouse said. "This is the driest thing I know. ' ... William the Conqueror, whose cause was favoured by the pope, was soon submitted to by the English ...' "

"That doesn't seem to be drying me," complained Alice.

"The best thing to dry us," the Dodo said, "would be a Caucus race."

"What is a Caucus-race?" asked Alice.

"The best way to explain it is to do it." The Dodo then marked out a race-course, in a sort of circle, and placed everyone along it, here and there. They all began running when they liked, and left off when they liked. At the end of half an hour, when everyone was quite dry, the Dodo called out suddenly, "The race is over!" "But who has won?" everybody asked.

"Why," said the Dodo, "everyone has won, and all must have prizes."

"But who is to give the prizes?"

"Why she, of course," the Dodo said, pointing to Alice. Alice put her hand in her pocket and found a box of comfits (luckily the salt-water had not got into it) and handed them round as prizes.

"But she must have a prize herself," said the Mouse.

"Of course," said the Dodo. "What else do you have in your pocket?" "Only a thimble," said Alice. She handed it to the Dodo, who then handed it back saying, "We beg your acceptance of this elegant thimble."

Alice thought the whole thing quite absurd, but they all looked so grave she didn't dare laugh. "I only wish my cat Dinah were here to see it," she said, but at this mention of a cat the birds, making different excuses, scattered as fast as possible in all directions.

Mushroom

FINISHED MEASUREMENTS

Height = 5in/13cm

Circumference around cap = 14in/35cm

MATERIALS

* Lion Brand Vanna's Choice 3.5oz[100g]/170yds[156m] (100% acrylic) – one skein each: #132 Radiant Orange (MC), #100 White (A), #171 Fern (B)

* Size H-8 (5mm) crochet hook OR SIZE TO OBTAIN GAUGE

* Tapestry needle

* Fiberfill stuffing

GAUGE

14 sc and 17 rows = 4in/10cm. TAKE TIME TO CHECK GAUGE.

Note: Stuff piece as it is worked to make stuffing easier.

MUSHROOM

Cap

Rnd 1: Using MC, 4 sc in magic ring, sl st to join, tighten magic ring – 4 sc.

Rnds 2–3, 5, 8: Ch 1, 2 sc in each st around, sl st to join.

Rnds 4, 6–7, 9, 11: Ch 1, sc in each st around, sl st to join.

Rnd 10: Ch 1, BLsc in each st around, sl st to join – 64 sc.

Rnd 12: Ch 1, sc2tog around, sl st to join – 32 sc.

Rnd 13: Using A, ch 1, sc in each st around, sl st to join – 32 sc.

Rnd 14: Ch 1, sc2tog around, sl st to join – 16 sc.

Rnd 15: Ch 1 sc in each st around, sl st to join – 16 sc.

Stem

Rnd 16: Using MC, ch 1, BLsc sc in each st around, sl st to join.

Rnd 17: Ch 1, sc in each st around, sl st to join.

Rnds 18–19, 22–23: Using B, ch 1, sc in each st around, sl st to join.

Rnds 20–21: Using MC, ch 1, sc in each st around, sl st to join.

Rnd 24: Ch 1, [sc in next st, 2 sc in next sc 8 times], sl st to join – 24 sc.

Rnd 25: Ch 1, [BLsc in next st, 2BLsctog] 8 times, sl st to join – 16sc.

Rnd 26: Ch 1, sc2tog 8 times, sl st to join – 8 sc.

Rnd 27: Ch 1, sc2tog 4 times, sl st to join – 4 sc. Fasten off, leaving tail.

FINISHING

Stuff lightly, stitch opening closed, weave in ends.

CHAPTER 6

Pig and Pepper

She stood looking at the house and wondering what to do next, when suddenly a footman in livery (with a face like a fish) came running out of the wood and rapped loudly at the door with his knuckles. It was opened by another footman in livery, with large eyes like a frog. Alice crept a little way out of the wood to listen.

The Fish-Footman began by producing from under his arm a great letter, nearly as large as himself, and this he handed over to the other, saying, in a solemn tone, "For the Duchess. An invitation from the Queen to play croquet." The Frog-Footman repeated, "From the Queen. An invitation for the Duchess to play croquet." Then they both bowed low, and their curls got entangled.

There was a most extraordinary noise going on inside the house —a constant howling and sneezing, and every now and then a great crash. Neither of the Footmen seemed the least helpful, so Alice timidly opened the door and went in.

The door led right into a large kitchen, which was full of smoke from one end to the other. The Duchess was sitting on a three-legged stool in the middle, nursing a baby; the cook was leaning over the fire, stirring a large cauldron which seemed to be full of soup.

"There's certainly too much pepper in that soup!" Alice said to herself, as well as she could for sneezing.

There was certainly too much of it in the *air*. Even the Duchess sneezed occasionally; and as for the baby, it was sneezing and howling alternately without a moment's pause. The only two creatures in the kitchen that did *not* sneeze were the cook and a large cat which was lying on the hearth and grinning from ear to ear.

"Please would you tell me," said Alice, "why your cat grins like that?"

"It's a Cheshire Cat," said the Duchess, "and that's why. Pig!"

She said the last word with such sudden violence that Alice quite jumped; but she saw in another moment that it was addressed to the baby, and not to her, so she took courage, and went on again: "I didn't know that cats *could* grin."

"You don't know much," said the Duchess, "and that's a fact."

At this point the cook took the cauldron of soup off the fire, and set to work throwing everything within her reach at the Duchess and the baby—the fire-irons, saucepans, plates, and dishes. The Duchess took no notice of them.

"Oh, *please* mind what you're doing!" cried Alice, jumping up and down in an agony of terror, as an unusually large saucepan flew past the baby's nose, nearly carrying it off.

"Oh, don't bother me!" said the Duchess. And with that she began nursing her child again, singing a sort of lullaby to it as she did so, and giving it a violent shake at the end of every line:

"Speak roughly to your little boy,
  And beat him when he sneezes:
He only does it to annoy,
  Because he knows it teases."

"Here! You may nurse it a bit, if you like!" the Duchess said to Alice, flinging the baby at her as she spoke. "I must go and get ready to play croquet with the Queen."

Alice caught the baby with some difficulty, as it was a queer-shaped little creature, and held out its arms and legs in all directions, "just like a star-fish," thought Alice. The poor little thing was snorting like a steam-engine when she caught it, and kept doubling itself up and grunting. "That's not a proper way of expressing yourself," said Alice.

The baby grunted again, and Alice looked very anxiously into its face. There could be no doubt that it had a very turned-up nose, much more like a snout than a real nose.

"If you're going to turn into a pig, my dear," said Alice seriously, "I'll have nothing more to do with you." It grunted again, so violently that she looked down into its face in some alarm. This time there could be no mistake about it; it was neither more nor less than a pig, and she felt that it would be quite absurd for her to carry it any further.

So she set the little creature down, and felt quite relieved to see it trot away quietly into the wood. "If it had grown up," she said to herself, "it would have made a dreadfully ugly child; but it makes rather a handsome pig, I think." She was startled to see the Cheshire Cat sitting on a bough of a tree a few yards off.

"Cheshire-Puss," she began, "which way should I go from here?"

"That depends a good deal on where you want to get to."

"I don't much care where—" said Alice.

"Then it doesn't matter which way you go," said the Cat.

"—so long as I get *somewhere*."

"Oh, you're sure to do that," said the Cat, "if you only walk long enough. In that direction," the Cat went on, "lives a Hatter—and in *that* direction lives a March Hare. They're both mad."

"But I don't want to go among mad people," Alice remarked.

"Oh, you can't help that. We're all mad here. By-the-bye, what became of the baby?"

"It turned into a pig," Alice answered very quietly.

"I thought it would," said the Cat, and vanished. A moment later it was back again, sitting on a branch of a tree.

"Did you say 'pig,' or 'fig'?" said the Cat.

"I said 'pig,'" replied Alice; "and I wish you wouldn't keep appearing and vanishing so suddenly: you make one quite giddy!"

"All right!" said the Cat; and this time it vanished quite slowly, beginning with the end of the tail, and ending with the grin, which remained some time after the rest of it had gone.

"Well! I've often seen a cat without a grin," thought Alice; "but a grin without a cat! It's the most curious thing I ever saw!"

She had not gone much farther before she came in sight of the house of the March Hare. She thought it must be the right house, because the chimneys were shaped like ears and the roof was thatched with fur.

There was a table set out under a tree in front of the house, and the March Hare and the Hatter were having tea at it: a Dormouse was sitting between them, fast asleep, and the other two were using it as a cushion, resting their elbows on it, and talking over its head.

"No room! No room!" they cried out when they saw Alice coming.

"There's plenty of room!" said Alice indignantly, and she sat down in a large armchair at one end of the table.

"Have some wine," the March Hare said in an encouraging tone.

"I don't see any wine," Alice said.

"There isn't any," said the March Hare.

"Then it wasn't very civil of you to offer it," said Alice angrily.

"It wasn't very civil of you to sit down without being invited," said the March Hare.

"Your hair wants cutting," said the Hatter.

"You should learn not to make personal remarks," Alice said. "It's very rude."

"And you should say what you mean," the March Hare went on.

"I do," Alice hastily replied; "at least—at least I mean what I say—that's the same thing, you know."

"Not the same thing a bit," said the Hatter. "You might as well say that 'I see what I eat' is the same thing as 'I eat what I see.' What day of the month is it?" he went on, looking at his watch and holding it to his ear.

Alice considered a little. "The fourth."

"Two days wrong!" sighed the Hatter. "I told you butter wouldn't suit the works!" he added, looking angrily at the March Hare.

"It was the best butter," the March Hare meekly replied.

"What a funny watch!" Alice remarked. "It tells the day of the month, and doesn't tell what o'clock it is!"

"Why should it?" muttered the Hatter. "Does *your* watch tell you what year it is?"

"Of course not," Alice replied: "but that's because it stays the same year for such a long time together."

"Which is just the same with mine," said the Hatter.

"Wake up, Dormouse!" the March Hare shouted, pouring tea on its nose, as the Hatter started to sing:

"Twinkle, twinkle, little bat!
How I wonder what you're at!
Up above the world you fly,
Like a tea tray in the sky.
Twinkle, twinkle —"

("Twinkle, twinkle, twinkle, twinkle —" sang the Dormouse sleepily.)

"I should think," Alice said, "you could find something better to do with your time—"

"Time?" the Hatter said. "We've nothing to do with Time. It's always six o'clock here."

"Is that the reason so many tea things are put out?" Alice asked.

"Yes, it's always tea-time, and we've no time to wash the things between whiles."

"Then you keep moving round, I suppose ?"

"Exactly so," said the Hatter: "as the things get used up."

"Take some more tea," the March Hare said to Alice.

"I've had nothing yet," Alice replied in an offended tone: "so I can't take more."

"You mean you can't take less," said the Hatter: "it's very easy to take *more* than nothing. I want a clean cup," he went on: "let's all move one place on."

He moved on as he spoke, and the Dormouse followed him: the March Hare moved into the Dormouse's place, and Alice rather unwillingly took the place of the March Hare, who had just upset the milk-jug.

"I don't think—" Alice began.

"Then you shouldn't talk," said the Hatter.

This piece of rudeness was more than Alice could bear: she got up in great disgust, and walked off. The Dormouse fell asleep instantly, and the last time she saw the other two, they were trying to put the Dormouse into the teapot.

"At any rate I'll never go *there* again!" said Alice. "It's the stupidest tea-party I ever was at in all my life!"

Just as she said this, she noticed that one of the trees had a door leading right into it. In she went, and once more found herself in the long hall, and close to the little glass table. She began by taking the little golden key, and unlocking the door that led into the garden. Then she went to work nibbling at the mushroom (she had kept a piece of it in her pocket) till she was about a foot high. Then she walked down the little passage: and *then*—she found herself at last in the beautiful garden, among the bright flower-beds and the cool fountains.

A large rose tree stood near the entrance of the garden: the roses growing on it were white, but there were three gardeners at it, busily painting them red. "Would you mind telling me, please," said Alice, "why you are painting these roses?"

Gardeners *Five* and *Seven* said nothing, but looked at *Two*. *Two* began in a low voice, "Why, the fact is, you see, Miss, this here ought to have been a *red* rose tree, and we put a white one in by mistake; and, if the Queen was to find it out, we should all have our heads cut off, you know." At this moment, *Five*, who had been anxiously looking across the garden, called out "The Queen! The Queen!" and the three gardeners instantly threw themselves flat upon their faces.

First came ten soldiers carrying clubs: these were all shaped like the three gardeners, oblong and flat, with their hands and feet at the corners; next the ten courtiers ornamented all over with diamonds. After these came the royal children, ornamented with hearts. Next came the guests, mostly Kings and Queens, and among them Alice recognized the White Rabbit. Then followed the Knave of Hearts, carrying the King's crown on a cushion, and last of all THE KING AND THE QUEEN OF HEARTS.

When the procession came opposite Alice, they all stopped and the Queen said: "Who is this? What's your name, child?"

"My name is Alice, so please your Majesty," said Alice; she added to herself, "Why, they're only a pack of cards, after all. I needn't be afraid of them."

The Queen pointed to the rose trees. "What's going on here?"

"How should I know?" said Alice. "It's no business of *mine*."

The Queen turned crimson with fury, and, after glaring at her for a moment like a wild beast, began screaming "Off with her head! Off with—"

"Nonsense!" said Alice, very loudly and decidedly.

"Can you play croquet?" the Queen asked after a long silence.

"Yes!" shouted Alice.

"Come on, then!" roared the Queen, and Alice joined the procession.

"It's—it's a very fine day!" said a timid voice at her side. She was walking by the White Rabbit, who was peeping anxiously into her face.

"Very," said Alice. "Where's the Duchess?"

"Hush! Hush!" said the Rabbit in a low hurried tone. He looked anxiously over his shoulder and whispered "She's under sentence of execution."

"What for?" said Alice.

"She boxed the Queen's ears—" the Rabbit began. Alice gave a little scream of laughter. "Oh, hush, the Queen will hear you!"

"Get to your places," shouted the Queen in a voice of thunder, and people began running about in all directions. However, they got settled down in a minute or two and the game began.

Alice thought she had never seen such a curious croquet ground in her life; it was all ridges and furrows. The croquet balls were live hedgehogs, and the mallets live flamingoes, and the soldiers had to double themselves up and stand on their hands and feet to make the arches.

The chief difficulty Alice found at first was in managing her flamingo: she succeeded in getting its body tucked away, comfortably enough under her arm, with its legs hanging down, but generally, just as she had got its neck nicely straightened out, and was going to give the hedgehog a blow with its head, it *would* twist itself round and look up in her face. When she had got its head down, and was going to begin again, it was very provoking to find that the hedgehog had unrolled itself, and was in the act of crawling away.

The players all played at once, without waiting for turns, quarreling all the while, and fighting for the hedgehogs; and in a very short time the Queen was in a furious passion, and went stamping about, and shouting, "Off with his head!" about once in a minute.

Alice was looking about for some way of escape, when she was surprised to see the Duchess coming.

"You can't think how glad I am to see you again, you dear old thing!" said the Duchess, as she tucked her arm affectionately into Alice's, and they walked off together.

Alice was very glad to find her in such a pleasant temper, and thought to herself that perhaps it was only the pepper that made her so savage when they met in the kitchen. "Maybe it's always pepper that makes people hot-tempered," she thought, "and vinegar that makes them sour —and barley-sugar and such things that make children sweet-tempered."

"You're thinking about something, my dear," the Duchess was saying, "and that makes you forget to talk. I'll remember the moral of that in a bit."

"Perhaps it hasn't one," Alice ventured to remark.

"Tut, tut, child!" said the Duchess. "Everything's got a moral, if only you can find it."

Alice did not much like her keeping so close to her, first because the Duchess was *very* ugly; and secondly, because she was exactly the right height to rest her chin on Alice's shoulder, and it was an uncomfortably sharp chin.

"The game's going on rather better now," said Alice, as she put down her flamingo.

" 'Tis so," said the Duchess: "and the moral of that is—'Take care of the sense, and the sounds will take care of themselves.' "

"How fond she is of finding morals in things!" Alice thought to herself.

"I make you a present," the Duchess said, "of everything I've said as yet."

"A cheap sort of present!" thought Alice.

To Alice's great surprise, the Duchess's voice died away, and there stood the Queen in front of them, with her arms folded, frowning like a thunder-storm.

"A fine day, your Majesty!" the Duchess began in a low, weak voice.

"Now, I give you fair warning," shouted the Queen; "either you or your head must be off! Take your choice!"

The Duchess took her choice, and was gone in a moment.

"Let's go on with the game," the Queen said to Alice; and Alice was too frightened to say a word. By the end of half an hour, all the players except the King, the Queen, and Alice were under sentence of execution.

Then the Queen left off, and said to Alice, "Have you seen the Mock Turtle yet?"

"No," said Alice. "I don't even know what a Mock Turtle is."

"It's the thing Mock Turtle Soup is made from," said the Queen. "Come on and he shall tell you his history."

As they walked off together, Alice heard the King say in a low voice to the company generally, "You are all pardoned." "Come, *that's* a good thing!" she said to herself, for she had felt quite unhappy at the number of executions the Queen had ordered.

They soon came upon a Gryphon, lying fast asleep in the sun. "Up, lazy thing!" said the Queen, "and take this young lady to see the Mock Turtle," and she walked off, leaving Alice alone with the Gryphon.

The Gryphon sat up and rubbed its eyes. "What fun!" it said.

"What *is* the fun?" said Alice.

"Why, *she*," said the Gryphon. "It's all her fancy: they never executes nobody, you know. Come on!"

They had not gone far before they saw the Mock Turtle in the distance, sitting sad and lonely on a little ledge of rock, and, as they came nearer, Alice could hear him sighing as if his heart would break. "What is his sorrow?" she asked the Gryphon. And the Gryphon answered,

"It's all his fancy, too: he hasn't got no sorrow, you know."

So they went up to the Mock Turtle, who looked at them with large eyes full of tears, but said nothing.

"This here young lady," said the Gryphon, "she wants to know your history, she do."

"I'll tell it to her," said the Mock Turtle in a deep, hollow tone. "Sit down, both of you, and don't speak a word till I've finished."

"Once," the Turtle said, with a deep sigh, "I was a real Turtle." These words were followed by a very long silence, broken only by an occasional "Hjckrrh!" from the Gryphon, and the constant heavy sobbing of the Mock Turtle. "When we were little," he went on, "we went to school in the sea. The master was an old Turtle—we used to call him Tortoise—"

"Why did you call him Tortoise, if he wasn't one?" Alice asked.

"We called him Tortoise because he taught us," said the Mock Turtle angrily. "Really you are very dull." They both looked at poor Alice, who felt ready to sink into the earth.

"We went to school in the sea, though you mayn't believe it—"

"I never said I didn't!" interrupted Alice.

"You did," said the Mock Turtle.

"I've been to a day-school, too," said Alice. "We learned French and music."

"And washing?" said the Mock Turtle.

"Certainly not!" said Alice indignantly.

"Now at *ours*," the Mock Turtle said, "they had 'French, music, *and washing*.' "

"You couldn't have wanted it much," said Alice, "living at the bottom of the sea."

"I couldn't afford to learn it," said the Mock Turtle with a sigh. "I only took the regular course."

"What was that?" inquired Alice.

"Reeling and Writing, to begin with—and then the different branches of Arithmetic —Ambition, Distraction, Uglification, and Derision."

"What else had you to learn?" said Alice.

"Well, there was Mystery," the Mock Turtle replied. "Mystery, ancient and modern, with Seaography, then Drawling—"

"I went to the Classical master," said the Gryphon. "He was an old crab, *he* was. He taught Laughing and Grief, they used to say."

"And how many hours a day did you do lessons?" said Alice.

"Ten hours the first day; nine the next; and so on."

"What a curious plan!" exclaimed Alice.

"That's the reason they're called lessons," the Gryphon remarked: "because they lessen from day to day."

"That's enough about lessons," he went on. "Tell her about the games now."

Sobs choked the Mock Turtle's voice. "You may not have lived much under the sea, or been introduced to a lobster, or known what a delightful thing a Lobster-Quadrille is!"

"What sort of dance is that?" said Alice.

"Why, you first form into a line along the sea-shore—" Without more ado, the Mock Turtle and the Gryphon began solemnly dancing round Alice (every now and then treading on her toes) as the Mock Turtle sang, very slowly and sadly—

"Will you walk a little faster?" said a whiting to a snail,
"There's a porpoise close behind us, and he's treading on my tail.
See how eagerly the lobsters and the turtles all advance.
They are waiting on the shingle—will you come and join the dance?
Will you, won't you, will you, won't you, will you join the dance?
Will you, won't you, will you, won't you, won't you join the dance?"

Alice was glad when the dance was over.

"Do you know why the whiting is called a whiting?" the Gryphon said. "Because it does the boots and shoes."

"Mine are done with blacking—"

"Well, under the sea the boots and shoes are done with whiting."

"And what are they made of?" Alice asked.

"Soles and eels, of course. Any shrimp could have told you that."

At this point the Mock Turtle, once more choked with sobs, began singing again:

> *"Beautiful Soup, so rich and green,*
> *Waiting in a hot tureen!*
> *Who for such dainties would not stoop?*
> *Soup of the evening, beautiful Soup!*
> *Soup of the evening, beautiful Soup!*
>
> *"Beau-ootiful Soo-oop!*
> *Beau-ootiful Soo-oop!*
> *Soo-oop of the e-e-evening,*
> *Beautiful, beautiful Soup!"*

He had just begun to repeat it when a cry, "The trial's beginning," was heard in the distance.

"Come on!" cried the Gryphon, taking Alice by the hand before she could ask whose trial it was.

The King and Queen of Hearts were seated on their throne when they arrived, with a great crowd assembled about them—all sorts of little birds and beasts as well as the whole pack of cards: the Knave was standing before them, in front of a table filled with tarts, and near the King was the White Rabbit, holding a trumpet.

Alice had never been in a court of justice before, but she had read about them in books, and she knew nearly everyone there. "That's the Judge," she said to herself, "because of his great wig." The Judge was the King; and as he wore his crown over the wig, he did not look at all comfortable.

"And that's the jury-box," thought Alice; "and those twelve creatures" (some were animals and some were birds) "are the jurors." She said this word two or three times, being rather proud of it.

The twelve jurors (one of whom proved to be Bill the Lizard) were busily writing on slates. "What are they doing?" Alice whispered to the Gryphon.

"They're putting down their names, for fear they should forget them before the end of the trial."

"Herald, read the accusation!" said the King. The White Rabbit blew three blasts on the trumpet, unrolled a scroll, and read:

"The Queen of Hearts, she made some tarts,
All on a summer day:
The Knave of Hearts, he stole those tarts
And took them quite away."

The first witness was the Hatter. He came in with a teacup in one hand and a piece of bread-and-butter in the other. "I beg pardon, your Majesty," he began, "but I hadn't quite finished my tea."

"You ought to have finished. When did you begin?"

The Hatter looked at the March Hare and the Dormouse. "Fourteenth of March, I think it was."

"Fifteenth," said the March Hare.

"Sixteenth," said the Dormouse.

"Write that down," the King said to the jury; and the jury wrote down all three dates on their slates, and then added them up, and reduced the answer to shillings and pence.

"Take off your hat," the King said to the Hatter.

"It isn't mine," said the Hatter.

"*Stolen!*" the King exclaimed.

"I keep them to sell," the Hatter added. "I've none of my own. I'm a hatter." He was trembling so he shook off both his shoes.

Just at this moment Alice felt a curious sensation: she was beginning to grow larger again, but she decided to remain where she was as long as there was room for her.

"I wish you wouldn't squeeze so," said the Dormouse, who was sitting next to her.

"I can't help it," Alice said very meekly. "I'm growing."

"You've got no right to grow *here*."

"Don't talk nonsense," said Alice more boldly: "you know you're growing too."

"Yes, but *I* grow at a reasonable pace," said the Dormouse.

"Give your evidence," the King ordered the Hatter, "or I'll have you executed."

The miserable Hatter dropped his teacup and bread-and-butter and went down on one knee. "I'm a poor man, your Majesty."

"You're a *very* poor *speaker*," said the King. "If that's all you know about it, you may stand down."

"I can't go no lower," said the Hatter: "I'm on the floor, as it is."

"Then you may *sit* down," the King replied.

The Hatter hurriedly left the court, without even waiting to put his shoes on.

"Call the *next* witness," the King said, when the court was cleared again. And he added, in an undertone to the Queen, "Really, my dear, *you* must cross-examine the next witness. It quite makes my forehead ache!"

Imagine Alice's surprise when the White Rabbit read out, at the top of his shrill little voice, "Alice!"

Rnd 4: Ch 1, [sc in next st, 2 sc in next st] around, sl st to join – 30 sc.

Rnd 5: Ch 1, sc in next 10 sts, 2 sc in each of next 2 sc, sc in next st, 2 sc in each of next 2 sc, sc in next 14 sts, 2 sc in each of next 2 sc, sc in next st, 2 sc in each of next 2 sc, sc in next 4 sts, sl st to join – 40 sc.

Begin Stripe pattern: 1 rnd A, 2 rnds MC.

Rnd 6: Using A, ch 1, BLsc in each st around, sl st to join – 40 sc.

Rnd 7: Using MC, ch 1, sc in next 19 sts, [ch 4, sk 3 for leg opening, sc in next 6 sts] 2 times, sc in next 3 sts, sl st to join.

Rnd 8: Using MC, ch 1, sc in next 19 sts, 3 sc in ch-sp, sc in next 6 sts, 3 sc in ch-sp, sc in next 9 sts, sl st to join – 40 sc.

Rnds 9, 12, 15, 18: Using A, ch 1, sc in each st around, sl st to join.

Rnds 10, 13, 16: Using MC, ch 1, sc in each st around, sl st to join.

Rnd 11: Using MC, ch 1, [sc in next 6 sts, sc2tog] around, sl st to join – 35 sc.

Rnd 14: Using MC, ch 1, [sc in next 5 sts, sc2tog] around, sl st to join – 30 sc.

Rnd 17: Using MC, ch 1, [sc in next 4 sts, sc2tog] around, sl st to join – 25 sc.

Rnd 19: Using MC, ch 1, sc2tog, sc in next 4 sts, sc2tog, sc in next st, ch 4, sk 3 for armhole, sc in next 8 sts, ch 4, sk 3 for armhole, sc in next 2 sts, sl st to join – 23 sc.

Rnd 20: Using MC, ch 1, sc in next 7 sts, 3 sc in ch-sp, sc in next 8 sts, 3 sc in ch-sp, sc in next 2 sts. Fasten off, leaving tail. Stuff and sew opening closed.

Arms (make 2)

Rnd 1: Using MC, 4 sc in magic ring, sl st to join, tighten magic ring, – 4 sc.

Rnd 2: Ch 1, 2 sc in each st around, sl st to join – 8 sc.

Rnd 3: Ch 1, sc in each st around, sl st to join.

Rnds 4–10: Work even in stripe pattern.

Rnd 11: Using B, ch 1, sc in each st around, sl st to join.

Rnd 12: Ch 1, sc2tog around – 4 sc. Fasten off, leaving tail. Sew opening closed. Sew to body at rnd 19 as illustrated.

Legs (make 2)

Rep Rnds 1–11 of Arms

Rnds 12–13: Ch 1, sc in each st around, sl st to join.

Rnd 14: Ch 1, sc2tog around – 4 sc. Fasten off, leaving tail. Sew opening closed. Sew to body at rnd 7 as illustrated.

Tail

Rnd 1: Using A, 4 sc in magic ring, sl st to join, tighten magic ring, turn – 4 sc.

Rnd 2: Using MC, ch 1, 2 sc in each of next 4 sts, sl st join – 8 sc.

Rnd 3: Ch 1, sc in each st around, sl st to join.

Rnds 4–25: Work even in stripe pattern. Fasten off, leaving tail. Stuff and sew to back of body.

Ears (make 2)

Row 1: Using MC, ch 2, sc in 2nd ch from hook, turn – 1 sc.

Row 2: Ch 1, 3 sc in next st, turn – 3 sc.

Row 3: Ch 1, 2 sc in next st, 3 sc in next st, 2 sc in next st, turn – 7 sc.

Row 4: Ch 1, sc in each st across, turn.

Row 5: Ch 1, sc in next st, 2 sc in next st, sc in next 3 sts, 2 sc in next sc, sc in next st, turn – 9 sc.

Rows 6–7: Ch 1, sc in each st across, fasten off, turn.

Row 8: Join A in back loop of 2nd st from edge, ch 1, BLsc in same st and in next 6 sts, turn – 7 sc.

Row 9: Ch 1, sc in each st across, turn.

Row 10: Ch 1, [sc in next st, sc2tog] 2 times, sc in next st, turn – 5 sc.

Row 11: Ch 1, sc in next st, sc3tog, sc in next st, turn – 3 sc.

Row 12: Ch 1, sc3tog. Fasten off, leaving a tail. Fold back pink inner part of ear and sew to orange outer ear. Sew ears to head as illustrated.

FINISHING

Weave in ends. Sew head to body.

Face

Referring to illustration, using 2 strands of embroidery floss, embroider outline sts for eyes, nose, mouth and whiskers. Fill in mouth with 2 rows of chain st using white yarn. Using B, embroider 3 rows of chain st for head marking lines.

Dormouse

FINISHED MEASUREMENTS

Length (without tail) = 4$^1/_2$ in / 11cm

Circumference = 5$^1/_2$ in / 14cm

MATERIALS

* Rowan Pure Wool Superwash Worsted 3.53oz[100 g] / 219 yds / 200m (100% superwash wool) – one skein each: #103 Almond (MC), #102 Soft Cream (A), #122 Plum (B) and small amounts of pink and black

* Size G-6 (4mm) crochet hook OR SIZE TO OBTAIN GAUGE

* Tapestry needle

* Fiberfill stuffing

GAUGE

16 sc and 20 rows = 4in / 10cm. TAKE TIME TO CHECK GAUGE.

DORMOUSE

Rnd 1: Using pink, 4 sc in magic ring, sl st to join, tighten magic ring – 4 sc.

Rnd 2: Using A, ch 1, [sc in next st, 2 sc in next st] 2 times, sl st to join – 6 sc.

Rnd 3: Ch 1, [sc in next st, 2 sc in next st] 3 times, sl st to join – 9 sc.

Rnd 4: Using MC, ch 1, [sc in next 2 sts, 2 sc in next st] 3 times, sl st to join – 12 sc.

Rnd 5: Ch 1, [sc in next 2 sts, 2 sc in next st] 4 times, sl st to join – 16 sc.

Rnd 6: Ch 1, [sc in next 3 sts, 2 sc in next st] 4 times, sl st to join – 20 sc.

Rnds 7, 10, 12, 15: Ch 1, sc in each st around, sl st to join.

Rnd 8: Using B, ch 1, sc2tog 2 times, 2 sc in next st, sc in next 10 sts, 2 sc in next st, sc2tog 2 times, sl st to join – 18 sc.

Rnd 9: Ch 1, sc in next 3 sts, 2 sc in each of next 2 sc, sc in next 3 sts, sc2tog, sc in next 3 sts, 2 sc in each of next 2 sts, sc in next 3 sts, sl st to join – 21 sc.

Rnd 11: Ch 1, sc in next st, [sc in next 4 sts, 2 sc in next st] 3 times, sc in next 5 sts, sl st to join – 24 sc.

Rnd 13: Using MC, ch 1, [sc in next 4 sts, sc2tog] 4 times, sl st to join – 20 sc.

Rnd 14: Ch 1, sc in next st, [sc2tog, sc in next 3 sts] 3 times, sc2tog 2 times, sl st to join – 15 sc.

Rnd 16: Ch 1, [sc in next st, sc2tog] 5 times, sl st to join – 10 sc.

Rnd 17: Ch 1, sc2tog 5 times, sl st to join – 5 sts. Fasten off, leaving tail. Stuff and sew opening closed.

Legs (make 1)

Ch 13, sc in 2nd ch from hook, sc in next st, sl st in next 8 sts, sc in next 2 sts, fasten off. Using crochet hook, pull legs through bottom of body as in photo.

Arms (make 1)

Ch 11, sc in 2nd ch from hook, sc in next st, sl st in next 6 sts, sc in next 2 sts, fasten off. Using crochet hook, pull legs through bottom of body as in photo.

Tail

Using MC, ch 16, sl st in 2nd ch from hook and each st across, fasten off and sew to back end of mouse.

Ears (make 2)

Using MC, work the following sts in magic ring - 2 sc, 3 hdc, 2 sc, switch to pink, sc, sl st to join, tighten magic ring, fasten off. Using tail of pink, fold pink sc and stitch to outer ear. Sew ears to head.

FINISHING

Weave in ends. Use black yarn to make a French knot eye on either side of head.

Mad Hatter

FINISHED MEASUREMENTS

Height (without hat) = 8¹/₂ in / 22cm

MATERIALS

* Rowan Pure Wool Superwash Worsted 3.53oz[100 g]/219 yds/200m (100% superwash wool) -one skein each: – #102 Soft Cream (MC), # 109 Black(A), #118 Candy(B), #121 Morello(C), #176 Teal Wash(D), #178 Green Wash(E)

* Rowan Mohair Haze .88 oz[25 g]/112 yds/102m (70% super kid mohair, 30% extra fine merino) -one skein: #535 Smile (F)

* Small amounts 6-strand embroidery floss in pink and black

* Paper for tag in hat

* Size G-6 (4mm) crochet hook OR SIZE TO OBTAIN GAUGE

* Tapestry needle

* Fiberfill stuffing

GAUGE

19 sc and 20 rows = 4in/10cm using MC. TAKE TIME TO CHECK GAUGE.

Note: Stuff doll as it is worked to make stuffing easier to. Do not stuff arms.

MAD HATTER

Feet

Rnd 1: Using A, 7 sc in magic ring, sl st to join, tighten magic ring, turn – 7 sc.

Rnd 2: Ch 1, sc in next st, 2 sc in each of next 5 sts, sc in next st, sl st to join, turn – 12 sts.

Rnd 3: Ch 1, sc in next 2 sts, (sc, hdc) in next st, 2 dc in next st, (dc, hdc) in next st, sc in next 2 sts, (hdc, dc) in next st, 2 dc in next st, (hdc, sc) in next st, sc in next 2 sts, sl st to join, turn – 18 sts.

Rnd 4: Ch 1, sc in next st, 2 sc in next st, sc in next st, hdc in next 2 sts, 2 dc in each of next 2 dc, hdc in next st, sc in next 2 sts, hdc in next st, 2 dc in each of next 2 dc, hdc in next 2 sts, sc in next sc, 2 sc in next sc, sc in next st, sl st to join, turn – 24 sts.

Rnd 5: Ch1, sc in next st, 2 sc in next st, sc in next 2 sts, hdc in next st , 2 hdc in next st, dc in next 2 sts, 2 dc in next st, hdc in next st, 2 hdc in next st, sc in next 2 sts, 2 hdc in next st, hdc in next st, 2 dc in next st, dc in next 2 sts, 2 hdc in next st, hdc in next st, sc in next 2 sts, 2 sc in next st, sc in next st, sl st to join, turn – 32 sts.

Rnd 6: Ch 1, BLsc in each st around, sl st to join, do not turn – 32 sts.

Rnd 7: Ch 1, sc in each st around, sl st to join.

Rnd 8: Ch 1, sc in next 7 sts, [sc2tog 4 times, sc in next 2 sts] 2 times, sc in next 5 sts, sl st to join – 24 sc.

Pants

Rnds 9 –16: Using D, ch 1, sc in each st around, sl st to join.

Shirt

Rnds 17–22: Using B, ch 1, sc in each st around, sl st to join.

Rnd 23: Ch 1, sc in next 3 sts, sc2tog, ch3, sk 2 for armhole, sc2tog, sc in next 6 sts, sc2tog, ch 3, sk 2 for armhole, sc2tog, sc in next 3 sts, sl st to join.

Rnd 24: Ch 1, sc in each sc and 2 sc in each ch-sp around, sl st to join – 20 sc.

Head

Rnd 25: Using MC, ch 1, BLsc in each st around, sl st to join.

Rnd 26: Ch 1, [sc in next 3 sts, sc 2 in next st] 5 times, sl st to join – 25 sts.

Rnd 27: Ch 1, [sc in next 4 sts, 2 sc in next st] 5 times, sl st to join – 30 sts.

Rnd 28: Ch 1, [sc in next 4 sts, 2 sc in next st] 6 times, sl st to join – 36 sts.

Rnds 29–34: Ch 1, sc in each st around, sl st to join.

Rnd 35: Using 2 strands of F, ch 1, sc in each st around, sl st to join.

Rnd 36: Ch 1, [sc in next 4 sts, sc2tog] 6 times, sl st to join – 30 sts.

Rnd 37: Ch 1, [sc in next 4 sts, sc2tog] 5 times, sl st to join – 25 sts.

Rnd 38: Ch 1, [sc in next 3 sts, sc2tog] 5 times, sl st to join – 20 sts.

Rnds 39–40: Ch 1, sc2tog around, sl st to join – 5 sts. Fasten off, leaving tail. Stuff and sew opening closed.

Arms (make 1)

Rnd 1: Using MC, 4 sc in magic ring, sl st to join, tighten magic ring, – 4 sc.

Rnd 2: Ch 1, 2 sc in each st around, sl st to join – 8 sc.

Rnds 3–30: Using B, ch 1, sc in each st around, sl st to join.

Rnd 31: Using MC, ch 1, sc in each st around, sl st to join.

Rnd 32: Ch 1, sc2tog 4 times, sl st to join – 4 sc. Fasten off, leaving tail. Sew opening closed. Pull arm piece through armholes, centering it so arms are of equal length. Weave in all ends.

Jacket

Row 1 (RS): Using C, ch 30, sc in 2nd ch from hook and each ch across, turn – 29 sc.

Row 2 (WS): Ch 1, sc in next 5 sts, ch 5, sk 5 for armhole, sc in next 9 sts, ch 5, sk 5 for armhole, sc in next 5 sts, sl st to join, turn.

Row 3: Ch 1, sc in next 5 sts, BLsc in next 5 ch, sc in next 9 sts, BLsc in next 5 ch, sc in next 5 sts, sl st to join, turn – 29 sc.

Row 4: Ch 1, sc in each st across, turn.

Row 5: Ch 1, sc in next 2 sts, (2 sc in next st, sc in next 3 sts) 6 times, 2 sc in next st, sc in next 2 sts, turn – 36 sts.

Rows 7–9: Ch 1, sc in each st across, fasten off, turn.

Collar

Row 10: Attach C in 6th sc from edge, sc in same st and in next 23 sts, turn - 24 sts.

Row 11: Ch 1, sc in next st, 2 sc in next st, sc in next 20 sts, 2 sc in next sc, sc in next st, fasten off.

Sleeves (make 2)

Rnd 1: With RS facing, join C to armhole, 5 sc in top of armhole, 1 sc in thread bet top and bottom, 5 sc in bottom of armhole and 1 sc in thread between top and bottom of armhole – 12 sc.

Rnd 2–13: Work even in sc.

Rnd 14: BLsc in each st around, sl st to join. Fasten off. Place jacket on doll. Use A to sew jacket closed with French knot buttons.

Hat

Rnd 1: Using E, 6 sc in magic ring, sl st to join, tighten magic ring, – 6 sc.

Rnd 2: Ch 1, [sc in next st, 2 sc in next sc] 3 times, sl st to join – 9 sc.

Rnd 3: Ch 1, 2 sc in each st around, sl st to join – 18 sc.

Rnd 4: Ch 1, [sc in next st, 2 sc in next st] 9 times, sl st to join – 27 sts.

Rnd 5, 8–10, 12–14, 16–20: Ch 1, sc in each st around, sl st to join.

Rnd 6: Ch 1, [sc in next 2 sts, 2 sc in next st] 9 times, sl st to join – 36 sts.

Rnd 7: Ch 1, [sc in next 5 sts, 2 sc in next st] 6 times, sl st to join – 42 sc.

Rnd 11, 15: Ch 1, [sc in next 4 sts, sc2tog] 6 times, sl st to join.

Rnd 21: Ch1, BLsc in each st around, sl st to join.

Brim

Rnd 22: Ch 1, [sc in next 2 sts, 2 sc in next sc] 10 times, sl st to join – 40 sc.

Rnd 23: Ch 1, [sc in next 3 sts, 2 sc in next sc] 10 times, sl st to join – 50 sc.

Rnd 24: Ch 1, [sc in next 4 sts, sc in next sc] 10 times, sl st to join – 60 sc.

Rnd 25: Ch 1, [sc in next 5 sts, 2 sc in next sc] 10 times, sl st to join – 70 sc. Fasten off.

FINISHING

Weave in ends, sew openings closed.

Hat Band

Row 1: Using A, ch 37, sc in 2nd ch from hook and each ch across, turn – 36 sc.

Row 2: Ch 1, sc in each st across, fasten off, sew into a ring. Place over hat.

Hair

Row 1: Using 2 strands F, ch 25, sc in 2nd ch from hook and each ch across, turn – 24 sc.

Row 2–5: Ch 1, sc in each st across, turn.

Row 6: Ch 1, sc in next sc, ch 5, sc in 3rd sc from hook 2nd unworked sc, [ch 1, turn, sc in sc just made, turn, ch 5, sc in 3rd sc (2nd unworked sc) from hook] across fasten off. Sew hair to head.

Necktie

Using D, ch 51, sc in 2nd ch from hook and each ch across, fasten off. Knot around neck.

Face

Using A, embroider eyes with a French knot surrounded by a lazy daisy st. Embroider mouth in chain st using 2 strands of pink floss. Embroider eyebrows in chain st using 2 strands of black floss.

Teapot and Cups

FINISHED MEASUREMENTS

Height = Teapot: $3^1/_2$ in/8.75cm (including lid); cup and saucer: $1^1/_4$ in/3.25cm

MATERIALS

* Rowan Pure Wool Superwash Worsted 3.53oz[100 g]/ 219 yds/200m (100% superwash wool) - one skein each: #146 Periwinkle (MC), #101 Ivory (A), #125 Olive(C), small amounts light and dark pink

* Small amounts 6-strand embroidery floss in green

* Size G-6 (4mm) crochet hook OR SIZE TO OBTAIN GAUGE

* Tapestry needle

* Fiberfill stuffing

* Stitch marker

GAUGE

19 sc and 20 rows = 4in/10cm. TAKE TIME TO CHECK GAUGE.

Note: Stuff piece as it is worked to make stuffing easier.

TEAPOT

Bottom

Rnd 1: Using MC, 6 sc in magic ring, sl st to join, tighten magic ring – 6 sc.

Rnd 2: Ch 1, 2 sc in each st around, sl st to join –12 sc.

Rnd 3: Ch 1, [sc in next st, 2 sc in next st] 6 times, sl st to join – 18 sc.

Rnd 4: Ch 1, [sc in next 2 sts, 2 sc in next st] 6 times, sl st to join – 24 sc.

Rnd 5: Ch 1, BLsc in each st around, sl st to join, pm.

Rnd 6: Ch 1, [sc in next 5 sts, 2 sc in next st] 4 times, sl st to join – 28 sc.

Rnd 7: Ch 1, sc in each st around, sl st to join.

Rnd 8: Ch 1, [sc in next 6 sts, 2 sc in next st] 4 times, sl st to join – 32 sc.

Divide for spout

Row 9: Ch 1, sl st in next st, [sc in next 5 sts, 2 sc in next st] 5 times, sl st in next st, turn – 35 sc.

Row 10: Ch 1, sc2tog, sc in next 31 sts, sc2tog, turn – 33 sc.

Row 11: Ch 1, sk sl st, sk sl st, sc in next 4 sts, [2 sc in next st, sc in next 7 sts] 3 times, 2 sc in next st, sc in next 4 sts, turn – 37 sc.

Row 12: Ch 1, sc in each st across, turn.

Rnd 13: Ch 1, sc in next 37 sts, ch 4, sl st in first sc of row to work in rnds.

Rnd 14: Ch 1, sc in next st, (sc in next 4 sts, sc2tog) 6 times, sc in each of 4 chs, sl st to join – 35 sc.

Rnd 15: Using B, ch 1, sc in next 5 sts, (sc2tog, sc in next 4 sts) 5 times, sl st to join – 30 sc.

Rnds 16–17: Using A, ch 1, sc in each st around, sl st to join.

Rnd 18: Using B, ch 1, sc in each st around, sl st to join.

Rnd 19: Using MC, ch 1, sc in each st around, sl st to join

Rnd 20: Working from left to right, reverse sc in each st around, sl st to join, fasten off.

Base

Rnd 1: Join MC to FL of base at marker in Rnd 5. Ch 1, (sc in next 2 sts, 2 sc in next st) 8 times, sl st to join – 32 sc.

Rnd 2: Working from left to right, reverse sc in each st around, sl st to join, fasten off.

Spout

Rnd 1: Join MC at center bottom of opening, sc 20 sts around, working 2 sts in each of 4 top sc, sl st to join – 20 sc.

Rnd 2: Ch 1, sc in each st around, sl st to join – 20 sc.

Rnds 3–4: Ch 1, hdc2tog 2 times, sc around to last 4 sts, hdc2tog 2 times, sl st to join – 12 sts.

Rnds 5–7: Ch 1, sc2tog, sc around to last 2 sts, sc2tog, sl st to join – 8 sc.

Rnds 8–10: Ch 1, sc in each st around, sl st to join. Fasten off.

Handle

Row 1: Using MC, ch 24, sc in 2nd ch from hook and each st across, turn – 23 sc.

Row 2: Ch 1, sc in each st across, fasten off and sew to teapot.

Lid

Rnd 1: Using B, 4 sc in magic ring, sl st to join, tighten magic ring – 4 sc.

Rnd 2: Ch 1, sc in each st around, sl st to join.

Rnds 3–4: Using MC, ch 1, 2 sc in each st around, sl st to join – 16 sc.

Rnd 5: Ch 1, [sc in next st, 2 sc in next st] 8 times, sl st to join – 24 sc.

Rnd 6: Ch 1, [sc in next 3 sts, 2 sc in next st] 6 times, sl st to join – 30 sc.

Rnd 7: Ch 1, [BLsc in next 3 sts, BLsc2tog] 6 times, sl st to join, fasten off.

FINISHING

Weave in ends. Use light pink to make a 5-petal lazy daisy flower with a French knot bud on each side. Embroider a French knot in the middle of the flower in dark pink.

Cups (make 3)

Rnd 1: Using MC, 6 sc in magic ring, sl st to join, tighten magic ring – 6 sc.
Rnd 2: Ch 1, 2 sc in each st around, sl st to join – 12 sc.
Rnd 4: Ch 1, [sc in next st, 2 sc in next st] 6 times, sl st to join –18 sc.
Rnds 4–7: Ch 1, sc in each st around, sl st to join – 18 sc. Do not fasten off.

Rnd 26: Ch 1, [sc in next st, sc2tog] 3 times, sl st to join – 6 sc.

Rnds 27: Ch 1, [sc in next st, sc2tog] 2 times, sl st to join. Fasten off, leaving long tail.

Pull arm piece through armholes, centering it so arms are of equal length. Weave in all ends.

Dress

Row 1: Using D, ch 27, sc in 2nd ch from hook and each st across, turn – 26 sts.

Row 2: Ch 1, Fl in next 5 sts, ch 3, sk 3 for armhole, FLsc in next 10 sts , ch 3, sk 3 for armhole, FLsc in next 5 sts, sl st to join, turn.

Rows 3: Ch 1, sc in 5 sts, sc in each of 3 chs, sc in 10 sts, sc in each of 3 chs, sc in 5 sts, turn – 26 sts.

Rows 4, 6: Ch 1, sc in each st across, turn.

Row 5: Ch 1, sc in next 3 sts, [2 sc in next st, sc in next 4 sts] 4 times, 2 sc in next st, sc in next 2 sts, turn – 31 sts.

Row 7: Ch 1, sc in next 3 sts, [2 sc in next st, sc in next 4 sts] 5 times, 2 sc in next st, sc in next 2 sts, turn – 37 sts.

Row 8: Ch 1, sc in each st across, sl st to join in the round.

Skirt

Rnd 9: Ch 1, sc in next 2 sts, [2 sc in next st, sc in next 7 sts] 4 times, 2 sc in next st, sc in next 2 sts, sl st to join – 42 sts.

Rnds 10–12, 14–16: Ch 1, sc in each st around, sl st to join.

Rnd 13: Ch 1, sc in next 4 sts, [2 sc in next st, sc in next 7 sts] 4 times, 2 sc in next st, sc in next 5 sts, sl st to join – 47 sts.

Rnd 17: Using D, BLsc, ch 2, BLsc in next st, sk 1 across, BLsc, ch2, BLsc in last st, sl st to join. Fasten off.

Neck Ruffle

Rnd 1: Join E at neck edge, sc in top of each ch to last 2 sts, sc2tog, turn – 25 sts.

Rnd 2: Ch 1, [2 sc in next st, sc in next st] 12 times, 2 sc in next last st, turn – 38sts.

Rnd 3: Ch 1, [(sc, ch 4, sc) in next st, sc in next st] 19 times. Fasten off.

Heart

Row 1: Using D, 5 sc in magic ring, sl st to join, tighten magic ring – 5 sc.

Row 2: Ch 1, *(sc, hdc, dc) in next st, (dc, hdc, sc) in next st**, (sc, ch2, sc) in next st, rep from * to **, turn.

Row 3: Ch1, (sc, hdc) in first st, 2 hdc in next st, (hdc, dc) in next st, (dc, hdc,) in next st, sc in next 3 sts, (sc, ch 2, sc) in ch-2 sp, sc in next 3 sts, (hdc, dc) in next st, (dc, hdc) in next st, 2 hdc in next st, (hdc, sc) in last st.

Fasten off, leaving long tail. Sew heart to Dress Bodice.

Headband

Row 1: Using D, ch3, sc in 2nd ch from hook and next st, turn – 2 sc.

Row 2: Ch 3, sc in next 2 sts, turn.

Rep Row 2 until headband is long enough to go around head. Fasten off and join ends into a circle.

Crown

Row 1: Using C, ch 3, sc in 2nd ch from hook and next st, turn – 2 sc.

Rows 2, 4, 6: Ch 4, sc in next 2 sts, turn.

Rows 3, 5, 7: Ch 1, sc in next 2 st, turn. Fasten off.

FINISHING

Weave in ends. Dress doll and sew back seam of dress.

Hair (Note that hair is made using 2 techniques. All hair is made with B.)

Cut 24 pieces of B 20in/51cm long. Starting in marked st, fold 2 strands in half and make a fringe knot in next 6 sts to the right and 6 to the left of center. These pieces will be pulled up to form the bun.

Make fringe by wrapping yarn 40 times around a piece of cardboard. With a separate piece of yarn, sl st 4 sts across the wrapped yarn, anchoring the strands. Fasten off. Cut the loops, keeping the 2 sides separate.

Sew the fringe section, sl st side down, to the center front of the doll's head. Smooth the hair and stitch down to the back of the head with 1-2 long anchoring sts. Fasten off. These sts will be covered by the hair that is pulled up to form the bun. Trim this fringe to about 1in/2.5cm longer than the row on the back of the head.

Smooth and pull up the back strands and stitch the knotted strands in a smooth flat bundle to the back of the head, using 1–2 anchoring sts. Wrap the ends into a topknot; stitch and wrap around the bun several times. Tuck in any loose pieces and secure.

Curl

Using B, embroider a split stitch curl on the forehead.

Anchor headband to head with a few small stitches; sew on crown.

Face

Follow the picture and make 2 straight stitch eyes. Embroider a straight stitch mouth using pink floss.

Embroider red cheeks by working 2 lazy daisy sts, one inside the other.

King of Hearts

FINISHED MEASUREMENTS

Height to top of head = $7^1/_2$ in / 18.5cm

MATERIALS

* Lion Brand Vanna's Choice 3.5oz[100g]/170yds[156m] (100% acrylic) - one skein each: #098 Lamb (MC), #153 Black (A), #124 Toffee (B), #113 Scarlet (C), #149 Silver Grey (D), # 100 White (E), #157 Radiant Yellow (F)

* Lion Brand Homespun 6oz[170g]/185yds[169m] (98% acrylic, 2 % other fiber) - one skein #601 Desert Mountain (G)

* Size H-8 (5mm) crochet hook OR SIZE TO OBTAIN GAUGE

* Tapestry needle

* Fiberfill stuffing

GAUGE

14 sc and 17 rows = 4in/10cm. TAKE TIME TO CHECK GAUGE.

Note: Stuff doll as it is worked to make stuffing easier. Do not stuff arms.

KING OF HEARTS

Feet

Rnd 1: Using A, 8 sc in magic ring, sl st to join, tighten magic ring, turn – 8 sc.

Rnd 2: Ch 1, [sc in next st, 2 hdc in each of next 2 sts, sc in next st] 2 times, sl st to join, turn – 12 sts.

Rnd 3: Ch 1, [sc in next st, hdc in next st, 2 hdc in each of next 2 sts, hdc in next st, sc in next st] 2 times, sl st to join, turn – 16 sts.

Rnd 4: Ch 1, sc in next 4 sts, 2 hdc in each of next 3 hdc, sc in next 2 sts, 2 hdc in each of next 3 hdc, sc in next 4 sts, sl st to join, turn – 22 sts.

Rnd 5: Ch 1, BLsc in each st around, sl st to join.

Rnds 6–7: Ch 1, sc in each st around, sl st to join.

Body

Rnd 8: Using A, ch 1, sc in each st around, sl st to join.

Rnd 9: Ch 1, sc in next 3 sts [2 sc in next st, sc in next 2 sts] 3 times, sc in next st, [2 sc in next st, sc in next 2 sts] 3 times, sl st to join – 28 sts.

Rnds 10–12, 14: Ch 1, sc in each st around, sl st to join.

Rnds 13: Ch 1, sc in next 3 sts [sc2tog, sc in next 2 sts] 3 times, sc in next st, [sc2tog, sc in next 2 sts] 3 times, sl st to join, turn – 22 sts.

Rnd 15: Ch 1, sc in next 5 sts, sc2tog, sc in next 9 sts, sc2tog, sc in next 4 sts, sl st to join, turn – 20 sts.

Rnd 16: Using MC, ch 1, sc in next 4 sts, sc2tog, sc in next 8 sts, sc2tog, sc in next 4 sts, sl st to join, turn – 18 sts.

Rnd 17: Ch 1, sc in next 4 sts, sc2tog, sc in next 7 sts, sc2tog, sc in next 3 sts, sl st to join, turn – 16 sts.

Rnd 18: Ch 1, [sc in next 3 sts, ch 2, sk 2 for armhole, sc in next 3 sts] 2 times, sl st to join.

Rnd 19: Ch 1, [sc in next 3 sts, sc in ch-sp, sc in next 3 sts] 2 times, sl st to join, turn – 14 sts.

Head

Rnd 20: Using MC, ch 1, [sc in next 2 sts, 2 sc in next st] 4 times, sc in next 2 sts, sl st to join, turn – 18 sts.

Rnd 21: Ch 1, sc in next 2 sts, 2 sc in next st, [sc in next 3 sts, 2 sc in next st] 3 times, sc in next 3 sts, sl st to join, turn – 22 sts.

Rnd 22: Ch 1, [sc in next 4 sts, 2 sc in next st] 4 times, sc in next 2 sts, sl st to join, turn – 26 sts.

Rnd 23: Ch 1, sc in next 2 sts, 2 sc in next st, [sc in next 6 sts, 2 sc in next st] 3 times, sc in next 2 sts, sl st to join, turn – 30 sts.

Rnds 24–27, 32, 34: Ch 1, sc in each st around, sl st to join, turn.

Rnd 28: Using B, ch 1, sc in next 2 sts, sc2tog, [sc in next 6 sts, sc2tog] 3 times, sc in next 2 sts, sl st to join –26 sts.

Rnd 29: Ch 1, [sc in next 4 sts, sc2tog] 4 times, sc in next 2 sts, sl st to join, turn – 22 sts.

Rnd 30: Ch 1, sc in next 2 sts, sc2tog, [sc in next 3 sts, sc2tog] 3 times, sc in next 3 sts, sl st to join, turn – 18 sts.

Rnd 31: Ch 1, [sc in next 2 sts, sc2tog] 4 times, sc in next 2 sts, sl st to join, turn – 14 sts.

Rnd 33: Ch 1, [sc in next st, sc2tog] 4 times, sc in next 2 sts, sl st to join, turn – 10 sts.

Rnd 35: Ch 1, sc in next st, sc2tog 4 times, sc in next st, sl st to join, turn – 6 sts. Fasten off, leaving tail. Stuff and sew opening closed.

Arms (make 1)

Rnd 1: Using MC, 4 sc in magic ring, sl st to join, tighten magic ring, – 4 sc.

Rnds 2, 6–8, 10–12, 14–16: Ch 1, sc in each st around, sl st to join.

Rnd 3: Using D, ch 1, sc in each st around, sl st to join.

Rnds 4–5: Ch 1, [sc in next st, 2 sc in next sc] around, sl st to join – 9 sc.

Rnds 9, 17, 18: Ch 1, [sc in next st, sc2tog] around, sl st to join.

Rnd 13: Ch 1, [sc in next st, 2 sc in next sc] 3 times, sl st to join – 9 sc.

Rnds 19–20: Using MC, ch 1, sc in each st around, sl st to join – 4 sc. Fasten off.

Robe (starting at top)

Row 1 (RS): Using C, ch 23, sc in 2nd ch from hook and each ch across, turn – 22 sc.

Row 2 (WS): Ch 1, sc in next 4 sts, ch 3, sk 3 for armhole, sc in next 8 sts, ch 3, sk 3 for armhole, sc in next 4 sts, sl st to join, turn.

Row 3 Ch 1, sc in next 4 sts, BLsc in next 3 ch, sc in next 8 sts, BLsc in next 3 chs, sc in next 4 sts, sl st to join, turn.

Rows 4, 6, 8–10, 12–13: Ch 1, sc in each st across; turn.

Row 5: Ch 1, sc in next 3 sts [2 sc in next st, sc in next 4 sts] 3 times, 2 sc in next st, sc in next 3 sts, turn – 26 sts.

Row 7: Ch 1, sc in next 2 sts, [2 sc in next st, sc in next 6 sts] 3 times, 2 sc in next st, sc in next 2 sts, turn –30 sts.

Row 11: Ch 1, sc in next 2 sts, [2 sc in next st, sc in next 4 sts] 5 times, 2 sc in next sc, sc in next sts, turn – 36 sts.

Edging

With RS facing, sc evenly around sides, working 1 sc in corner, 11 sc along front edge, 2 sc in corner, 20 sc across neck, 2 sc in corner, 11 sc along front edge, 2 sc in corner, 36 sc across bottom, sl st to join. Fasten off.

With RS facing, join E at bottom of front edge, sc in each st around. Fasten off.

With RS facing, join D in bottom corner st, sc in 36 bottom sts and 1 corner st. Fasten off.

Sleeves (make 2)

Rnd 1: With RS facing, join C to armhole, ch1, [sc in next 2 sts, 2 sc in next st] 2 times, sl st to join – 8 sc.

Rnd 2: Ch 1, [sc in next 3 sts, 2 sc in next st] 2 times, sl st to join – 10 sc.

Rnd 3: Ch 1, [sc in next 4 sts, 2 sc in next st] 2 times, sl st to join – 12 sc.

Rnd 4: Ch 1, [sc in next 5 sts, 2 sc in next st] 2 times, sl st to join – 14 sc.

Rnds 5–6: Ch 1, sc in each st around, sl st to join. Fasten off.

Wig

Rnd 1: Using G, 5 sc in magic ring, sl st to join, tighten magic ring – 5 sc.

Rnds 2–3: Ch 1, 2 sc in each st across, sl st to join – 20 sc.

Rnd 4: Ch 1, [sc in next st, 2 sc into next sc] across, sl st to join – 30 sc.

Beg working in rows for hair.

Row 5: Ch 1, [sc in next 2 sts, 2 sc in next st] 7 times, sc in next 2 sts, turn, leaving 7 sts unworked – 30 sc.

Rows 6–15: Ch 1, sc in each st across, turn. Fasten off.

Crown

Using F, ch 26, sl st to join rnd.

Rnd 1: Ch 1, sc in each st around, sl st to join.

Rnd 2: Ch 1, BLsc in each st around, sl st to join.

Rnd 3: Ch 1, [sl st in next st, hdc in next st, (dc, tr, dc) in next st, hdc in next st, sl st in next st] 5 times, sl st to join. Fasten off.

Heart

Using C, 2 hdc, sc, ch 2, sc, 2 hdc, ch 1 in magic ring, sl st to join, tighten magic ring. Fasten off.

FINISHING

Block lightly, weave in ends. Embroider face as illustrated. Pull arm piece through armholes, centering it so arms are of equal length. Weave in all ends. Tack wig to head and crown to top of wig. Place robe on doll.

Flower Pot and Rose Bush

FINISHED MEASUREMENTS

Height = 4in/10cm

MATERIALS

* Lion Brand Vanna's Choice 3.5oz[100g]/170yds[156m] (100% acrylic) - one skein each: #171 Fern (MC), #124 Toffee (A) and small amounts of #172 Kelly Green (B), #100 White (C), #113 Scarlet (D)

* Small amounts 6-strand embroidery floss in pink for mouth and cheeks

* Size H-8 (5mm) crochet hook OR SIZE TO OBTAIN GAUGE

* Stitch markers

* Tapestry needle

* Fiberfill stuffing

GAUGE

14 sc and 17 rows = 4in/10cm. TAKE TIME TO CHECK GAUGE.

Note: Stuff piece as it is worked to make stuffing easier.

FLOWER POT

Bottom

Rnd 1: Using A, 6 sc in magic ring, sl st to join, tighten magic ring – 6 sc.

Rnd 2: Ch 1, [sc in next st, 2 sc in next st] 3 times, sl st to join – 9 sc.

Rnd 3: Ch 1, [sc in next st, 2 sc in next st] 4 times, sc in next sc, sl st to join – 13 sc.

Rnd 4: Ch 1, [sc in next st, 2 sc in next st] 6 times, sc in next st, sl st to join – 19 sc.

Rnd 5: Ch 1, BLsc in each st around, sl st to join.

Side

Rnd 6: Ch 1, [sc in next 2 sts, 2 sc in next st] 6 times, sc in next st, sl st to join – 25 sc.

Rnds 7–11: Ch 1, sc in each st around, sl st to join.

Rnd 12: Ch 1, sc in next 3 sts, 2 sc in next st, [sc in next 5 sts, 2 sc in next st] 3 times, sc in next 3 sts, sl st to join – 29 sc. Pm in this rnd.

Rim

Rnd 13: Ch 1, FLsc in next 4 sts, 2 FLsc in next st, [FLsc in next 6 sts, 2 FLsc in next st] 3 times, FLsc in next 3 sts, sl st to join – 33 sc.

Rnd 14: Ch 1, sc in each st around, sl st to join. Fasten off leaving long tail to sew rim down to pot.

ROSE BUSH

Join MC to inner edge of flower pot at marker from Rnd 12. Work this rnd in the BL of Rnd 12.

Rnd 1: Ch 1, BLsc in each st around, sl st to join – 29 sts.

Rnd 2: Ch 1, sc in next 4 sts, 2 sc in next sc, [sc in next 6 sts, 2 sc in next sc] 3 times, sc in next 3 sts, sl st to join – 33 sc.

Rnd 3: (Ruffle) Ch 1, FLsc in next 2 sts, (FLsc, FLhdc, FLsc) in next sc, [FLsc in next 6 sts, (FLsc, FLhdc, FLsc) in next st] 4 times, FLsc in next 2 sts, sl st to join.

Rnd 4: Work in back loops of Rnd 2. Ch 1, sl st into back loop of first st of Rnd 2, BLsc in each st around, turn.

Rnd 5: Ch 1, sc in next st, [sc in next 6 sts, sc2tog] 4 times, sl st to join – 29 sc.

Rnd 6: Ch 1, sc in each st around, sl st to join.

Rnd 7: Ch 1, sc in next 3 sts, sc2tog, [sc in next 4 sts, sc2tog] 4 times, sl st to join – 24 sc.

Rnds 8–9: Ch1, sc in each st around, sl st to join.

Rnd 10: Ch 1, [sc in next 2 sts, sc2tog, sc in next 2 sts] 4 times, sl st to join – 20 sc.

Rnds 11–12, 14, 16: Ch 1, sc in each st around, sl st to join.

Rnd 13: Ch 1, sc in next 2 sts, sc2tog, [sc in next 3 sts, sc2tog] 3 times, sl st to join – 16 sc.

Rnd 15: Ch 1, [sc in next 2 sts, sc2tog] 4 times, sc in next 2 sts, sl st to join – 12 sc.

Rnd 17: Ch 1, [sc in next 2 sts, sc2tog] 3 times, sl st to join – 9 sc.

Rnd 18: Ch 1, [sc in next 2 sts, sc2tog] 2 times, sc in next st, sl st to join – 7 sc.

Rnd 19: Ch 1, [sc in next st, sc2tog] 2 times, sc in next st, sl st to join – 5 sc.

Fasten off, leaving tail. Stuff and sew opening closed.

Roses (make 5 with C and 2 with D)

Ch 8, (sc, ch 1, sl st) in 2nd ch from hook and in each rem ch. Fasten off leaving tail. Coil into a flower shape and secure with a couple of sts.

Leaves (make 7)

Using B, ch 8, sc in 2nd ch from hook, hdc in next st, sl st in next 3 sts, hdc in next st, sc in next st. Fasten off leaving tail.

FINISHING

Sew Roses and Leaves onto Rose Bush as illustrated. Weave in ends.

Croquet Card Arch

SKILL LEVEL
Easy

FINISHED MEASUREMENTS

Height = 3in/7.5cm

MATERIALS

* Lion Brand Vanna's Choice 3.5oz[100g]/170yds[156m] (100% acrylic) - one skein each: #100 White (MC), #123 Beige (A) and small amounts of #153 Black (B), #113 Scarlet (C) , #172 Kelly Green (D)

* Small amounts 6-strand embroidery floss in pink and black

* Size H-8 (5mm) crochet hook OR SIZE TO OBTAIN GAUGE

* Tapestry needle

* Fiberfill stuffing

GAUGE

14 sc and 17 rows = 4in/10cm. TAKE TIME TO CHECK GAUGE.

CROQUET CARD ARCH

Card (worked from long side across)

Row 1: Using MC, ch 36, sc in 2nd ch from hook and each ch across, turn – 35 sts.

Rows 2–15: Ch 1, sc in each st across, turn. Fasten off.

Arches (make 2)

Row 1: Using A, ch 7, sc in 2nd ch from hook and next 5 sts, ch 1, working in other side of ch, sc in next 6 sts, turn – 13 sts.

Row 2: Ch 1, sc in next 6 sts, 2 sc in ch, sc in next 6 sts, turn – 14 sts.

Row 3: Ch 1, sc in next 6 sts, 2 sc in each of next 2 sc, sc in next 6 sts, turn – 16 sts.

Row 4: Ch 1, sc in next 6 sts, 2 sc next st, sc in next st, ch 1, sc in next st, 2 sc in next st, sc in next 6 sts, turn – 19 sts.

Row 5: Ch 1, sc in next 7 sts, 2 sc next st, sc in next st, sc in ch-sp, sc in next st, 2 sc in next sc, sc in next 7 sts, fasten off – 21 sts.

Diamond Face (make 2)

Row 1 (RS) : Using B, ch 7, sc in 2nd ch from hook, next 5 sts, turn – 6 sc.

Rows 2, 4, 6, 8, 10, 12 (WS) : Ch 1, sc in next st, switch to A with yarn in front, sc in next 5 sts, turn.

Rows 3, 5, 7, 9, 11: Ch 1, sc in next 5 sts, switch to B with yarn in back, sc in next st, turn.

Row 13: Using B, ch 1, sc in each st across, fasten off.

Black Diamonds (make 2)

Row 1: Using B, ch 6, sc in 2nd ch from hook and next 4 sts, turn – 5 sc.

Rows 2–5: Ch 1, sc in each st across, turn. Fasten off.

Small Diamond (make 2)

Row 1: Using B, ch 3, sc in 2nd ch from hook and next st, turn – 2 sc.

Row 2: Ch 1, sc in each st across. Fasten off.

Hands and Feet (make 2)

Rnd 1: Using D, ch 17, sc in 2nd ch from hook and next 15 sts, ch 1, working in other side of ch, sc in next 16 sts, ch 1, sl st to join, fasten off – 33 sts.

FINISHING

Weave in ends.

Fold face in half and stitch around edges. Use 6 strands of embroidery floss to embroider straight stitch eyebrows, colonial knot eyes, and a straight stitch mouth. Using pink floss, embroider straight stitch cheeks.

Sew diamonds to card piece. Use 6 strands of embroidery floss to embroider stem stitch number 2 at bottom of card.

Fold card in half and mark top fold. Matching top of fold to top of arches, sew in arches to each side of card. Fold excess card fabric under the arches, stuff with fiberfill, and close seam.

Sew hands and feet pieces to bottom of stuffed card. Sew on face.

Flamingo Mallet

SKILL LEVEL
Intermediate

FINISHED MEASUREMENTS

Height from top tuft = $7^1/_4$ in/18cm

MATERIALS

* Lion Brand Vanna's Choice Baby 3.5oz[100g]/170yds[156m] (100% acrylic) - one skein each: #138 Pink Poodle (MC), #139 Berrylicious (A), #100 White (B), #153 Black (C)

* Size H-8 (5mm) crochet hook OR SIZE TO OBTAIN GAUGE

* Tapestry needle

* Fiberfill stuffing

GAUGE

14 sc and 17 rows = 4in/10cm. TAKE TIME TO CHECK GAUGE.

Note: Stuff doll as it is worked to make stuffing easier. Do not stuff arms.

FLAMINGO MALLET

Rnd 1: Using MC, 5 sc in magic ring, sl st to join, tighten magic ring – 5 sc.

Rnd 2: Ch 1, 2 sc in each st around, sl st to join – 10 sc.

Rnd 3: Ch1, BLsc in each st around, sl st to join.

Rnds 4–12: Ch 1, sc in each st around, sl st to join.

Rnds 13–14: Using A, ch 1, sc in each st around, sl st to join.

Rnd 15: Using MC, ch 1, [sc in next st, 2 sc in next st] 5 times, sl st to join – 15 sc.

Rnd 16: Ch 1, sc in each st around, sl st to join.

Divide for head

Row 17: Ch 1, sc in next 14 sts, turn – 14 sc.

Row 18: Ch 1, sc in next 5 sts, sc2tog 2 times, sc in next 5 sts, turn – 12 sc.

Row 19: Ch 1, sc in next 4 sts, sc2tog 2 times, sc in next 4 sts, turn – 10 sc.

Row 20: Ch 1, sc in next 3 sts, sc2tog 2 times, sc in next 3 sts, turn – 8 sc. Fasten off.

Beak

Rnd 1: With right side facing, join MC at top of right-hand side of head opening, work 4 sc down this side, sc in rem sc from neck, work 4 sc along other side, sl st to join – 9 sc.

Rnd 2: Ch 1, sc in each st around, sl st to join.

Rnd 3: Using C, ch 1, sc in each st around, sl st to join.

Rnd 4: Ch 1, [sc in next sc, sc2tog] 3 times – 6 sc.

Rnd 5: Using A, ch 1, sc in each st around, sl st to join.

Rnd 6: Ch 1, sc in next st, sc2tog 2 times, sc in next st, sl st to join – 4 sc.

Rnd 7: Ch 1, sc in each st around, sl st to join. Fasten off, leaving tail. Stuff and sew opening closed.

FINISHING

Sew top of head seam; weave in ends. Using C, embroider French knot eyes.

Neck Ruff

Cut 2 pieces of A 6in/15cm long;, fold in half and make a fringe knot through a sc at the neck edge. Repeat all around neck. Trim ruff and fluff yarn using tapestry needle.

Top Tuft

Cut 5 pieces of A 6 in/15 cm long. Fold yarn in half, make a fringe knot at the top of the head, trim yarn, and fluff with tapestry needle.

Hedgehog Ball

FINISHED MEASUREMENTS

Height = $2^{1}/_{2}$ in / 6cm

MATERIALS

* Lion Brand Vanna's Choice 3.5oz[100g]/170yds[156m] (100% acrylic) - one skein # 123 Beige (MC), small amount of #153 Black

* Lion Brand Homespun 6oz[170g]/185yds[169m] (98% acrylic, 2 % other fiber) - one skein #601 Desert Mountain (A)

* Sizes H-8 (5mm) and I-9 (5.5mm) crochet hooks OR SIZE TO OBTAIN GAUGE

* Tapestry needle

* Fiberfill stuffing

GAUGE

14 sc and 17 rows = 4in/10cm using smaller hook. TAKE TIME TO CHECK GAUGE.

Note: Stuff doll as it is worked to make stuffing easier.

HEDGEHOG BALL

Rnd 1: Using A and larger hook, 5 sc in magic ring, sl st to join, tighten magic ring, – 5 sc.

Rnd 2: Ch 1, 2 sc in each st around, sl st to join – 10 sc.

Rnd 3: Ch 1, [2 sc in next st, sc in next st] 5 times, sl st to join – 15 sc.

Rnd 4: Ch 1, sc in next st, 2 sc in next st, [sc in next 2 sts, 2 sc in next sc] 4 times, sc in next st, sl st to join – 20 sc.

Rnds 5–6: Ch 1, sc in each st around, sl st to join – 20 sc.

Rnd 7: Ch 1, sc in next st, sc2tog, [sc in next 2 sts, sc2tog] 4 times, sc in next st, sl st to join – 15 sc.

Rnd 8: Using MC and smaller hook, ch 1, sc in each st around, sl st to join.

Rnd 9: Ch 1, [sc2tog, sc in next st] 5 times, sl st to join – 10 sc.

Rnd 10: Ch 1, sc in each st around, sl st to join.

Rnd 11: Ch 1, sc2tog 5 times, sl st to join – 5 sc.

Rnd 12: Ch 1, sc in each st around, sl st to join. Fasten off, leaving tail. Stuff and sew opening closed.

Ears (make 2)

Using A and smaller hook, ch 2, 3 sc in 2nd ch from hook; fasten off, leaving tail. Sew ears to body as illustrated.

FINISHING

Using black yarn, embroider a French knot nose and 2 French knot eyes.